Alok Ranjan completed his B.A. (Hons) in economics from St. Stephen's College, Delhi. Thereafter, he did his MBA from Indian Institute of Management Ahmedabad (IIMA). Before retiring as chief secretary to the government of Uttar Pradesh, he had a long 38-year career with the Indian Administrative Service (IAS), having joined in 1978.

During his career, Ranjan served as a district magistrate, and collector, municipal commissioner, general manager as well as managing director of public sector corporations. He served as secretary/principal secretary to the government of Uttar Pradesh in the departments of education, finance, urban development and environment.

Ranjan also served as secretary to the chief minister as well as agriculture production commissioner and infrastructure and industrial development commissioner of Uttar Pradesh. He also worked as joint secretary of the Ministry of Defence and managing director of National Agricultural Cooperative Marketing Federation of India Ltd (NAFED).

Ranjan is a skilled writer who contributes essays on topics pertaining to public policy and leadership to prestigious national newspapers such as *The Times of India*, *Economic Times*, *Business Standard* and *The Pioneer* in addition to writing a regular column for the *Millennium Post*. In an effort to give back to society and share his experiences with others, he has also written several books.

He is an acclaimed thought leader and public speaker and takes regular sessions on leadership and management at IIM Lucknow and Jaipuria Institute of Management, Lucknow. He has also been speaking regularly on leadership, public policy and good governance at the National Centre for Good Governance and other administrative training institutes. Ranjan is an independent director on the board of various companies and academic institutions. He also mentors civil service aspirants.

Praise for the Book

"*Beyond GDP* is a rare book that treats happiness as a serious subject for economics and governance. Drawing on global research, Indian experience and world happiness reports, Alok Ranjan shows why GDP and income are too narrow to guide public policy and how a focus on well-being can correct that bias. The sections on the Easterlin Paradox, social capital and mental health are particularly persuasive in explaining why fast-growing societies like India can still feel anxious and discontented. This is a timely framework for policymakers, administrators and citizens who want development to be measured by how people actually live and feel, not just by how much they produce. A must-read for all those in quest of happiness."

Amitabh Kant, former CEO of NITI Aayog and G20 Sherpa

"Here is another gem from Alok Ranjan. With his vast experience as a civil servant, he brings forth in his book how governments, through appropriate policy formulation and effective implementation can impact happiness of the people. He rightly believes that good governance is a major determinant of the level of happiness of its people. For him, apart from other things, good governance is primarily minimum government and maximum governance, a supportive government and not an intrusive one. This well-researched book not merely examines various aspects of governance and its relationship with happiness but also prescribes how governance can contribute to people's happiness."

Anil Swarup IAS (Retd),
former secretary, School Education, GoI
former secretary, Coal, GoI,
author and public speaker

"In this timely and reflective work, Alok Ranjan, a seasoned Indian civil servant, challenges the dominance of GDP as the primary measure of progress and makes a compelling case for happiness and well-being as the true goals of public policy. Drawing on global frameworks such as the human development index, gross national happiness and the world happiness reports—alongside India's own governance experience—the book offers a lucid, humane and deeply grounded perspective on development. Blending lived administrative insight with ethical reflection, it provides a sobering corrective to the tendency to equate economic growth with social progress. Clear, thoughtful and anchored in both data and values, the book argues persuasively that public policy must ultimately be judged by its impact on people's happiness and life satisfaction, making it an essential read for policymakers, scholars and citizens concerned with the deeper purpose of governance."

Prof. Debashis Chatterjee,
director, Indian Institute of Management Kozhikode

"*Beyond GDP* is a deeply thoughtful and timely work that challenges the conventional obsession with GDP as the sole measure of progress. Drawing from his vast administrative experience and rigorous scholarship, Alok Ranjan makes a compelling case for placing human well-being and life satisfaction at the heart of public policy. The book masterfully weaves together global frameworks such as HDI, SDGs, world happiness reports and Bhutan's Gross National Happiness, while grounding the discussion firmly in the Indian context. What stands out is the author's clarity, balance and moral conviction—recognizing the importance of economic growth, yet reminding us that growth without equity, dignity and happiness is hollow. This book is not merely an academic contribution; it is a policy manifesto for humane governance. It should be essential reading for policymakers, civil servants, scholars and anyone committed to building a more compassionate and people-centric state."

Dr Himanshu Rai,
director, Indian Institute of Management Indore

"Alok Ranjan has produced a gem of a book with an orientation of public policymaking with the focus on happiness of the people. He gets away from the old mould of judging a public policy on the shibboleth of economic growth or of achievement of SDGs. According to him, public policy has to be citizen centric and should be judged on the basis of happiness it produces, creating an ecosystem where the community and the government act in tandem to make citizens happy and contented. After an analysis of the contemporary thoughts on development, he opts for judging governance through the prism of a new happiness index. An excellently written book which should engender fresh thinking in policymakers."

Yogendra Narain IAS (Retd),
former chief secretary, government of Uttar Pradesh,
former defence secretary, GoI,
former secretary general, Rajya Sabha

BEYOND GDP

In Pursuit of Measuring HAPPINESS

ALOK RANJAN

Om Books International

First published in 2026 by

Om Books International

Corporate & Editorial Office
A-12, Sector 64, Noida 201 301
Uttar Pradesh, India
Phone: +91 120 477 4100
Email: editorial@ombooks.com
Website: www.ombooksinternational.com

Sales Office
107, Ansari Road, Darya Ganj,
New Delhi 110 002, India
Phone: +91 11 4000 9000
Email: sales@ombooks.com
Website: www.ombooks.com

ISBN: 978-93-6395-488-5

Printed in India

10 9 8 7 6 5 4 3 2 1

"The care of human life and happiness, and not their destruction, is the first and only object of good government."

Thomas Jefferson

To

a future scenario where everyone can aspire to a life of purpose, meaning and happiness

Contents

Introduction

सर्वे भवन्तु सुखिनः सर्वे सन्तु निरामयाः ।
सर्वे भद्राणि पश्यन्तु मा कश्चिद्दुःखभाग्भवेत ।।
ऊँ शान्तिः शान्तिः शान्तिः

"Sarve Bhavantu Sukhinah
Sarve santu niramayah
Sarve bhadrani pasyantu ma kascidduh
Khabhagbhaveta"
(May all be happy.
May all be healthy
May all look to the good of others)

—*Brihadaranyaka Upanishad*

I designed and taught a course on happiness to MBA students of Jaipuria Institute of Management, Lucknow. I analysed happiness from the point of view of psychologists, sociologists, economists and spiritual seekers. This book deals with the happiness aspects of economic development and expansion. The book's main argument is that public policy should prioritize people's quality of life, which is based on their degree of happiness, rather than just growth rates and related data. Even at the international level the erstwhile Washington Consensus, which primarily emphasizes market-driven growth, has been replaced by the London Consensus which prioritizes inclusivity and institutional strength.[1]

In May 2023, a group of 55 scholars met at the London School of Economics and arrived at five fundamental principles to direct policymaking for the 21st century. The foremost among these principles was that there should be a focus on well-being that goes beyond GDP and money incomes. It should seek to incorporate self-worth, social status, unity and other non-materialistic conceptions of well-being. It also seeks to make growth a matter of gaining the trust of the citizens which would come only if they are content. This book hopes to establish happiness as the ultimate goal of public policy.

Every country in the world is pursuing the goal of a certain GDP growth rate and trying to showcase the GDP data as an indicator of development and progress.

---

1. The Washington Consensus refers to a set of 10 economic policy prescriptions that emerged in the late 1980s, primarily aimed at developing countries facing economic crises. The key principles were market liberalization, privatization, fiscal discipline and property rights. In contrast, the London Consensus is a newly proposed framework developed in the 21st century, spearheaded by economists at the London School of Economics. It aims to address the shortcomings of the Washington Consensus by focusing on inclusive development, institutional resilience and multidimensional approach.

Governments celebrate high growth rates and the media carries impressive headlines about quarterly or annual GDP numbers. There is, in fact, an obsession with GDP which is projected as the ultimate indicator of a country's prosperity. However, there is life beyond GDP, which is a purely economic indicator, and does not indicate whether the people of a nation are living happily and healthily. Even when two countries have comparable GDP per capita and high growth rates, we find that people's quality of life differs. In one country, people could be living healthy and secure lives having faith in their community and institutions, while the situation could be exactly the opposite in the other country. This book acknowledges the value of GDP as a growth indicator but not as a measure of everything that matters in life, hence it is necessary to develop and assess alternative indicators of progress and improved life satisfaction.

Beyond GDP dwells upon happiness as being the ultimate goal of every human being and brings fore arguments and evidence to show that GDP growth rate accounts for only a small portion of happiness, which is much more than growth in production and consumption of goods and services. Happiness would mean that the people of a nation enjoy a sustained sense of well-being and a high level of life satisfaction. It is towards this that nations and their policy makers must direct their energies. Recently the chief economic advisor to the Government of India stated that the GDP growth rate is crucial but it needs to have a purpose. To my mind this purpose must be the happiness and well-being of the people.

In order to understand how policies can be tailored to instil happiness and a high degree of life satisfaction in people, this book attempts to study other measures of human development and conducts a thorough analysis of the state of happiness worldwide as reported in the world happiness reports. The central idea is to focus on the quality of life.

GDP was never meant to be a measure of well-being when it was developed in the 1930s and 1940s as a tool to quantify economic production. Even the architect of GDP, Simon Kuznet was clear that it cannot be used as a proxy for human welfare. He warned against equating national income with societal welfare, emphasizing that GDP measures economic activity rather than overall well-being. The later adoption and widespread use of GDP as a primary measure of progress were driven by other factors (ease of calculation, political expediency, the Cold War focus on economic growth) that often overshadowed Kuznets's original caveats.

This book traces the evolution of economics over the ages starting from Greek philosophy till the present day. Originally a branch of philosophy, economics was preoccupied with the human situation and saw human happiness and well-being as the goal to strive for. But with the advent of materialism in the 20th century, economics evolved into a discipline that examined the production and consumption of goods and services. The focus shifted away from humans who became just another factor of production like land or capital whose productivity had to be increased in the interest of higher growth rate. This approach ignored the fact that the human being is far more than a resource.

GDP takes into consideration all expenditures even if they may be leading to social or ecological breakdown. It ignores the fact that there could be a big gap between economic growth and the lived reality of the people. While GDP measures production, consumption, income, output and various forms of expenditure, it does not reveal anything about mental health, social cohesion, environmental loss, inequality or happiness and life satisfaction. This explains the phenomenon that rising GDP can often coexist with widening inequality, job insecurity, ecological stress, erosion of trust and loneliness.

This anomaly is highlighted by the paradox put out by economist Richard Easterlin, which is thoroughly examined in this book. Easterlin demonstrated that more growth does not inevitably lead to better lives. Growth is important but it is not enough on its own. There is in urgent need to move beyond GDP. The pandemic has revealed that a high GDP does not guarantee resilience. Further, the scourge of climate change has sharply exposed the cost of ignoring sustainability. We are living in the age of AI and technological disruption which will not only transform the world but also threaten jobs, dignity and meaning. Above all, wealthy societies are facing an epidemic of loneliness and mental health crises.

In the outstanding book *Together: The Healing Power of Human Connection in a Sometimes Lonely World*, former US Surgeon General Dr Vivek Murthy observes that loneliness is a major public health issue in the United States and adds unequivocally that loneliness has a significant impact on people's general well-being. It contributes to anxiety, depression, addiction, violence and other social problems. He says that loneliness triggers stress responses that are harmful for the body over time. Lack of intimate relationships, poor social support and a lack of a feeling of community are all signs of loneliness. It is directly co-related with heart disease, dementia and weaker immunity leading even to premature death. GDP would never be able to explain how loneliness affects life satisfaction. Because of this, gauging a society's level of happiness is essential.

The central thesis of David Courtwright's book *The Age of Addiction: How Bad Habits Became Big Business* is that global capitalism has systemically targeted the brain's reward and motivation systems, which he refers to as the limbic system, encouraging excessive consumption and habituation to a wide range of substances and experiences, including tobacco, alcohol, gambling, processed foods, and digital products like social media and videogames. The so-called "invisible hand" of capitalism operates beyond the confines of profit and markets. It also fosters specific ideologies—most notably those of individualism, materialism and competition—that slowly infiltrate our societal structures, becoming deep-seated elements of our cultural fabric.

The obsession with growth creates a consumerist society where desires are engineered and exploited to create dependence and addiction in the search for profit maximization. A GDP-focused evaluation of development would never take into account public health and policy responses to these addictions, which have a significant impact on people's well-being.

More than 40 per cent of Japanese adults reported feeling alone or socially isolated at some point in their lives, according to a government survey conducted in the country with a very high GDP. This is especially true given how quickly the population is ageing. There is limited time for interpersonal relationships due to long workdays and a rigorous workplace culture. Poor mental health outcomes are caused by a profound isolation from society. The Chinese growth story, which demonstrates a remarkable era of persistently high GDP growth rate since the 1990s, is lavishly praised by economists and other thought leaders. However, this development is not a pure blessing. According to studies, the degree of life satisfaction among Chinese citizens has decreased since 1990. According to the official coverage of China's Central Economic Work Conference in December 2025, President Xi Jinping urged policymakers and economists to focus more on "high quality development" instead of only chasing GDP growth numbers.

Jinping talked about addressing deeper structural imbalances related to productivity, technology adoption and employment quality which go beyond the traditional approach of mere GDP measurement. This reflected a strategic reorientation from chasing growth figures to building a robust, sustainable and modern economy.

India has been putting up a stellar performance regarding GDP growth rate in recent years, making it one of the fastest-growing economies of the world. As per recent media reports, India has overtaken Japan to emerge as the world's fourth-largest economy, and is poised to surpass Germany to become the third-largest by 2030, according to an official release. India might attain a level of 30 trillion-dollar GDP by 2047. Yet we cannot ignore the fact that as of 2024, India's per capita GDP was about $2700 per annum giving it a rank of 144th in the world. This indicates that we have to look beyond the GDP growth rate figures to understand the real level of development in India.

Given the aforementioned, it is not surprising that India is ranked in the bottom 10 percentile of both the global happiness index and the human development index. A lot of work needs to be done in the areas of education, health and employment generation to improve the quality of life of the people of India. The country should not only focus on GDP growth rates, but also on all other measures of inclusive and sustainable growth. Behavioural economics today is reinforcing the concept of happiness and well-being because it is being increasingly realized that economic growth alone does not guarantee greater happiness. Even though happiness is deemed to be too subjective, soft and difficult to measure, new methods of measuring happiness are evolving and presenting a more credible picture of life satisfaction. Governments are using data on happiness and well-being to determine success in public policy and governance. Happiness data that has evolved is statistically robust and predicts health, productivity and longevity, and complements economic metrics without replacing them.

The GDP and welfare lenses provide differing perspectives on contemporary issues. For example, from a GDP perspective, unemployment is a loss of income; nevertheless, from a well-being perspective, it is an issue of dignity and mental health. Similarly, from a GDP viewpoint, even AI and automation are productivity-related challenges, but from a well-being standpoint, it all comes down to people and their capacity for self-determination.

This book seeks to go beyond measuring GDP to pursue different measures of happiness. Joseph Stiglitz once said, "What we measure affects what we do. If we measure the wrong thing, we will do the wrong thing." This principle highlights the critical role of metrics in shaping policies and decisions. It is for this reason that the book postulates that people have to be at the heart of policymaking, and every aspect of public policy must be evaluated by the impact it has on the life satisfaction of the people. An effective policy should reflect the needs and aspirations of the community it serves and bring about better outcomes for all. The optimal policy is the one that correctly evaluates the quality of the life of the people and contributes to making it better.

If happiness were to become the goal of government, many local and national priorities may change, and the weights attached to various policies may shift. For example, treatment for mental health conditions may be considered just as important as treatment for physical ailments; improving non-monetary aspects of work would be seen as crucial alongside improving wages; and investments in social capital that generate cohesion and a sense of belonging may be given as much attention as investments in physical infrastructure.

But the path to happiness becoming the explicit goal for all governments is not straightforward. Governments may not always have the capability to deliver on this goal effectively. There is much work to be done in the next decade. For some countries, the next step may be to use happiness as a tool to prioritize policies that increase the well-being of their citizens. For others, the first step may be creating and cementing the institutions that can facilitate that process in the first place. If governments around the world can get it right, the next decade may just see a self-reinforcing cycle of happier people creating happiness for others.

1

The Economics of Happiness

Exploring the Paradox of Wealth and Well-Being

"He who is not contented with what he has, would not be contented with what he would like to have."—Socrates

GDP, along with the measures of happiness, is the most accurate assessment of people's quality of life. People desire to be happy and GDP growth by itself does not ensure that. It is for this reason that a large number of countries and the UN are now advocating happiness as a policy objective.

Happiness—a concern of economists

Happiness has been the central concern of economists for a long time. Robert Malthus, in his 1798 seminal work "An Essay on the Principle of Population", observed, "The professed object of Dr Adam Smith's inquiry is the nature and causes of the wealth of nations. There is another inquiry, however, perhaps still more interesting, which he occasionally mixes with it, it means an inquiry into the causes which affect the happiness of nations."

Adam Smith's views on happiness and economic growth are complex and multifaceted. While he was indeed concerned with the study of happiness, he was not an advocate of economic growth being able to generate happiness. Smith's work, particularly *The Wealth of Nations* (1776), emphasizes that wealth and happiness are not directly proportional. He believed that wealth can increase happiness, but it is not the sole determinant. Smith's perspective is nuanced, as he acknowledges that wealth can provide the necessities of life and contribute to social engagement and tranquility, which are vital components of happiness. Early in the 20th century, economists shifted their emphasis from happiness to the economic growth model. It was Richard Easterlin who in 1974 addressed this crucial issue of happiness, and his pathbreaking research served as the basis for happiness economics, which is now a thriving field.

Happiness as a goal in Greek philosophy

Economics, as a discipline, initially concerned itself with a study of ethics and moral philosophy. Ancient Greek philosophers were of the opinion that living a life of virtue and morality makes a person realize his purpose in life.

Socrates, the first moral thinker of Greek philosophy, believed that morality was important for a happy life. The pursuit of wealth and glory is not nearly as important as wisdom and morality.

Material goods, according to Socrates, do not lead to a meaningful life. Clearly, for him, the higher aspects of wisdom were of far greater relevance to life than acquisition of worldly possessions. His famous disciple Plato stated that pleasures are relative and often lead to pain and misery. True and enduring pleasure is found in the exercise of reason and in the possession of truth and goodness.

The greatest philosopher Aristotle was more pragmatic in his thinking. For him, happiness and virtue went together. A virtuous person would be a happy one. According to Aristotle, a life of reason is a joyful existence and reason is a unique human ability. Human passion should be subordinated to reason. A life devoted to sensual pleasures is not a happy one. However, Aristotle accepted that the external conditions of life have a bearing on happiness.

Wealth, friendships, health and good fortune contribute significantly to a sense of well-being. He recognized that poverty, sickness and misfortune will make even a virtuous man miserable. Aristotle advocated moderation and saw virtue as a mean between two extremes just as courage offers a middle ground between cowardice and recklessness. He also stated that the welfare of citizens is the objective of the state and people can be happy and virtuous only under it.

Roughly 300 years after Aristotle's death, Epicurus proposed a materialist philosophy. For him, happiness was an end by itself while pain was the only evil. His school of philosophy, Epicureanism, regarded the pursuit of happiness as the chief aim of life. It elaborated on the various aspects of happiness. Mental pleasure for him was superior to physical pleasure. After Epicurus came the stoic school of thought which focused on wisdom as a cardinal virtue and considered extreme views as unacceptable. The stoics believed that being virtuous, which was a responsibility, was the only path to happiness and that pleasure should be avoided.

The evolution of GDP as a measure of economic growth

As stated earlier, the early economists were interested in happiness and even Adam Smith doubted the role of material wealth in generating happiness. Although he acknowledged that material wealth was an important area for economists to study, he did not associate a rise in material wealth with greater happiness.

Imagine a world where every action you take is carefully considered to ensure it brings the greatest amount of happiness to the most people. This might sound like an idealistic vision, but it is the essence of Jeremy Bentham's philosophy of utilitarianism. Bentham, a prominent British philosopher and social reformer, developed the principle of utilitarianism, which has profoundly influenced ethical theory, economics and public policy. He was adamant that the pursuit of greater happiness is inherently desirable and that happiness is the ultimate objective of human existence.

The main tenet of utilitarianism was that people should aim at promoting "the greatest happiness for the greatest number". Happiness meant pleasure and absence of pain while unhappiness was a feeling of pain and deprivation of pleasure. However, such an outlook would not lead to a higher way of life.

John Stuart Mill countered this while making a distinction between higher and lower pleasures with higher pleasures being mental, aesthetic and moral. He believed that pleasures should be evaluated not only by their quantity but also by their quality, which involves the distinctively human faculties. Mill's utilitarianism emphasized that actions were right if they promoted happiness, and he argued that some pleasures, such as those derived from art and literature, were superior to lower pleasures that were primarily physical gratifications. However, utilitarians ignored the distributional aspects of happiness, meaning that while maximizing overall happiness is important, it may not be sufficient to address the distribution of that happiness among individuals. Critics argue that utilitarianism can lead to unjust outcomes, such as the suffering of a minority being justified by the greater pleasure of the majority.

The ideas of Bentham were incorporated in economics and the economists at that time were of the view that the happiness of the people is the factor which supports all policy decisions. Marshall's magnum opus *Principles of Economics*, published in 1890, explores happiness at multiple levels. Marshall's views on happiness are deeply intertwined with his concept of "well-being", which he defined as the sum total of all the elements that contribute to a person's happiness. He believed that happiness should be the primary goal of economics, not just the accumulation of wealth. Marshall's work on happiness in economic society emphasized the importance of freedom of work and the need to ensure that the poorest people benefit from this freedom. Marshall's approach to happiness was rooted in his belief that wealth is a tool for improving living conditions and reducing poverty, rather than a goal in itself.

Clearly Marshall along with other economists was concerned with addressing a deeper and more relevant issue—the happiness of human beings. Subsequently, economists began to focus on choice and gave less importance to the idea of happiness. They gave a highly sophisticated framework to examine decision-making and to explain the theory of price, quantity and equilibrium. Economics then evolved into a field that linked people's happiness to the production and use of goods.

They proclaimed that people would be better off if production and consumption increased. Economics, like the hard sciences, began to follow the scientific method and therefore gave lesser importance to subjective well-being (SWB). It was believed that greater income would lead to more satisfaction of needs and so greater well-being. GDP as a measure of growth is the result of this thinking.

American economist and government official, and one of the key thinkers in 20th-century development studies, W.W. Rostow, advocated that the final aspiration for any country should be to reach the age of high mass consumption. Other countries should model themselves after the West, aspiring to a "modern" state of capitalism and liberal democracy.

Using these ideas, Rostow penned his classic *Stages of Economic Growth* in 1960, which presented five steps through which all countries must pass to become developed: traditional society, preconditions to take-off, take-off, drive to maturity and age of high mass consumption. The model asserted that all countries exist somewhere on this linear spectrum and climb upward through each stage in the development process. Rostow believed that Western countries, most notably the United States, occupied this last "developed" stage. Here, a country's economy flourishes in a capitalist system, characterized by mass production and consumerism. Rostow's Stages of Growth model is one of the most influential development theories of the 20th century. It was published at the height of the Cold War, and with the subtitle "A Non-Communist Manifesto," which was overtly political.

Theorists have challenged this approach, emphasizing a "bottom-up" development paradigm, in which countries become self-sufficient through local efforts, and urban industry is not necessary. Rostow also assumed all countries have a desire to develop in the same way, with the end goal of high mass consumption, disregarding the diversity of priorities that each society held and the different measures of development. For example, while Singapore is one of the most economically prosperous countries, it also has one of the highest income disparities in the world.

Rostow disregarded one of the most fundamental geographical principles: site and situation. Rostow assumed all countries have an equal chance to develop, without regard to population size, natural resources, or location. Singapore, for instance, has one of the world's busiest trading ports, but this would not be possible without its advantageous geography as an island nation between Indonesia and Malaysia.

John Maynard Keynes's vision of happiness and economics is deeply rooted in his belief that material wealth is a necessary but not sufficient condition for enjoying a good life. He argued that happiness should be measured not just by income but also by the quality of life, leisure and the opportunities available to individuals. Keynes's work has been influential in the development of happiness economics, which seeks to understand the relationship between economic factors and subjective well-being.

Simon Kuznets famously stated, "Economic welfare cannot be adequately measured unless the personal distribution of income is known. And no income measurement undertakes to estimate the reverse side of income, that is, the intensity and unpleasantness of effort going into the earning of income. The welfare of a nation can, therefore, scarcely be inferred from a measurement of national income as defined above."

In 1955, Kuznets put forward the hypothesis that as economies developed, national inequality would first increase and then decrease—an inverted U-shape. He theorized the genesis of the curve as arising from the twin forces of structural transformation of the economy and political economy pressures. The Kuznets curve still has a hold on development discourse as new data is used to test the hypothesis, new theories are elaborated to explain the evolution of inequality and the metaphor of an inverse U-shape is extended beyond its original realm of national inequality.

Easterlin Paradox explained

Economists quickly discovered that while GDP is a useful indicator of the production and consumption of goods and services, it does not provide a comprehensive picture of people's well-being.

After World War II, industrialized countries experienced unprecedented economic growth that significantly improved people's living conditions. However, rising wealth did not result in rising well-being. This discrepancy was first identified in 1974 by Richard A. Easterlin after observing the American time series of GDP per capita and of subjective well-being. Subsequently, the absence of a correlation between economic growth and well-being became known as the Easterlin Paradox. He documented that the trend of SWB in the US had been flat despite sustained economic growth. He was then a professor of economics at the University of Pennsylvania.

Easterlin was an engineer by education and came to economics at a later stage but his background reflected in his scientific rigour even when analysing a subjective matter like general well-being. Easterlin studied the databases of surveys conducted in 19 countries over a period of several years to determine whether economic growth improved the well-being of human beings.

The Easterlin Paradox highlights the relationship between income and happiness, suggesting that while happiness may increase with income at a certain point, it does not necessarily trend upward over time. Thus, high-income individuals often experience greater levels of happiness than low-income individuals at any given time and within a specific nation. Similarly, countries with higher per capita income tend to report higher levels of happiness.

However, when you consider the situation over a time period you will find that there are no significant changes in people's happiness when income grows over time. Countries' average levels of happiness do not rise in tandem with economic expansion.

Easterlin concluded that there is no long-term correlation between income and happiness as a result of this.

The Easterlin Paradox has significantly influenced the field of economics and happiness research. It has led to a re-evaluation of how economic growth is measured and its impact on individual and societal happiness. The paradox has prompted researchers to explore the relationship between income, happiness and economic development, leading to a more nuanced understanding of what contributes to well-being. The paradox has also sparked discussions on the role of social comparison in happiness, the importance of long-term trends and the need for a more comprehensive approach to welfare economics. Subjective well-being research relies on people's own assessment of their happiness measured through opinion polls or questionnaires.

This highlighted the subjective evaluation of a person's well-being. It is incorrect to discuss objective happiness or objective wellness because happiness is a subjective term. Since every person is unique and has a different perspective on life, their values and standards are crucial in determining how well they are doing. Easterlin applied the fundamental economics idea that an individual has the only right to evaluate their own life. Happiness economics empowers people. Because of Easterlin's work, economists were compelled to reconsider how important it was to deal with real people and comprehend their unique circumstances.

It became clear that there was much more to life than money. Happiness research believes that the pursuit of happiness is the main goal of human action. Welfare economics does not adequately address the issue of well-being.

Economists had been concerned with the idea of progress and believed that the societies should aspire to an age of high mass consumption. This implied that the primary goal was to increase production, thereby treating people like machines. The Easterlin Paradox challenges this thinking by arguing that social progress must not be equated to economic growth. This was recognized by the UN in 2011. It acknowledged the pursuit of happiness as a fundamental human goal and the need for a more inclusive, equitable and balanced approach to economic growth that promotes sustainable development, poverty eradication, happiness and the well-being of all peoples. This new approach to well-being is of great importance to public policy.

An article by Caspar F. Kaiser and Maarten C.M. Vendrik in the book *The Economics of Happiness* (published in 2019), edited by Mariano Rojas, attempts to evaluate the Easterlin Paradox's applicability to Europe. They came to the conclusion that for a set of nine western and northern European nations, the Easterlin Paradox was confirmed in both the long and medium term. However, the results for a set of 11 East European countries did not satisfy this paradox.

Spain, Greece and Italy suggested a rejection of the paradox for the medium term. This can be correlated with the fact that western and northern European countries have a higher per capita GDP as compared to southern and eastern European countries. According to Kaiser and Vendrik's research, economic progress over the past 40 years has not increased average life satisfaction in higher-income European countries over the long or medium term. One argument could be that as people's income rises, they eventually adjust to it and their aspirations rise as well, which prevents pleasure from rising as much.

The relative income theory, which holds that people derive utility from income in comparison to other groups, offers an additional explanation. The relative income theory, proposed by James Duesenberry in 1949, suggests that individuals derive utility from their income in relation to others rather than just their absolute income. This theory posits that people are more concerned with their consumption and savings decisions based on their income relative to their peers, which can lead to increased spending on luxury goods to maintain or enhance social status.

Rojas discovered that relative income has a significant impact on people's well-being whereas absolute income had less of an impact in a study conducted for several Latin American countries. Furthermore, since our pleasure with any income level depends on the discrepancy between our expectations and actual income, expectations play a significant role in determining subjective well-being. Only when our real income is in line with our expectations can SWB rise.

Tibor Scitovsky, another economist, worked extensively in this field concurrently with Easterlin, and it might be argued that he too contributed to the paradox's discovery and proposed potential explanations. His findings were published in his seminal work *The Joyless Economy* (originally published in 1976) and other works. The book explores the relationship between consumer behaviour and human satisfaction. It argues that economic abundance does not necessarily lead to satisfaction and that people's need for stimulation is vital. Scitovsky's work has been influential in the field of behavioural economics, providing insights into the psychological aspects of consumer behaviour and the need for more satisfying experiences beyond mere consumption.

He also popularized the ideas of novelty and comfort. People can pursue life happiness in two ways: either by pursuing comfort as a means of achieving financial contentment, or by engaging in creative and stimulating activities where novelty is a crucial component that offers excitement and pleasure. The concept of novelty and comfort is central to understanding human satisfaction.

Scitovsky postulated that people seek both economic satisfaction and creative activities that stimulate and create pleasure. He argued that overindulging in comfort can lead to dissatisfaction in the long run, as true pleasure often requires effort and skill. This perspective highlights the importance of balancing comfort with stimulating activities to enhance overall satisfaction in life.

Novelty is likely to produce a long-lasting sense of well-being since it offers the thrill of discovering and learning something new, which further develops life skills. When given the choice between comfort and novelty, people typically opt for comfort due to inadequate education, which makes them less conscious, or overly rigid parenting during childhood, which prevents them from taking chances or being creative. According to the Easterlin Paradox, despite economic progress, SWB at the national level might not rise. If proper education for life skills is provided to people, they will become open to exploration and SWB may well rise along with economic growth. This could explain why some countries exhibit rising trends.

Empirical analysis of growth and social well-being

In a different chapter titled "Unhappiness as an Engine of Economic Growth" by Stefano Bartolini in *Economics of Happiness,* the author makes the case that India, the US and China which account for almost 40 per cent global of the population and have experienced high economic growth rate over the past few decades. The growth in the US has been at the top of the ladder. However, throughout the same time span, the levels of leisure, social capital and happiness of citizens in these countries significantly decreased.

According to the author, social failure and economic achievement coexist in these nations. In these countries, social well-being has decreased, working hours have increased, social capital has declined and materialism has increased. Each of these nations exemplifies the Easterlin Paradox.

According to the author's research, India's average life satisfaction per decile decreased in 2014 when compared to 1990. In both these years, higher income brought more satisfaction but each income decile experienced lower levels of happiness than in 1990. Average life satisfaction fell by 25 per cent.

Between 1990 and 2007, the average life satisfaction in China decreased by 7 per cent. China's GDP per capita expanded fourfold during that time, lifting over half a billion people out of extreme poverty and raising life expectancy from 67 to 73.5 years, making the fall in SWB in China and India quite unexpected. The India story was also similar. In western Europe, there was a small rise in both wealth and happiness during the same time period.

Despite the remarkable growth in the US during this period there has been a sharp increase in the use of psychiatric drugs. Since the 1970s, SWB has drastically decreased in the US. Depression and other mental illnesses have been on the rise. There has been an increase in cases of drug addiction and overuse also. The suicide rate in the US has also been increasing. Similar is the experience in China and India.

Loneliness has become a major problem in the US as families have become unstable with fewer marriages and more divorces. The China story has been comparable. It is not that social capital, that is, the quality and quantity of a person's connections to other people and the community, always declines with rising economic growth. This is demonstrated by instances from other nations. Nearly 70 per cent of Chinese and 50 per cent of Americans are under a lot of pressure to be successful and make more money.

This leads to lower SWB as materialistic individuals give a higher priority to life goals such as making more money, creating an image and achieving a certain status and this is affected by one's relative position. Working hours have also increased a lot in the US, India and China though they have diminished in western Europe, placing a great deal of strain on family life.

The disturbing global trend of depleting social capital

Materialism is on the rise in most parts of the world and this is not a happy trend. It implies that people are experiencing poorer social capital, as the pursuit of material wealth often comes at the expense of social connections and community. The constant comparison and desire for more can result in envy, dissatisfaction and a lack of genuine happiness. Materialism can also lead to stress and anxiety, especially during the holidays when the focus shifts to material gifts. It drives unsustainable consumption patterns, depleting resources and causing environmental harm. Additionally, materialism can weaken personal relationships by prioritizing work and financial success over spending quality time with family and friends. Of course, different nations have varying degrees of materialism.

All this is leading to a social crisis in the US, China and India. I think defensive growth (my coinage) could be the explanation. Defensive growth means that money is a defence whether real or illusory against poverty of social capital. This strategy makes up for a lack of fulfilling relationships by consuming more or achieving greater success or status in life. Market goods and services replaced non-market sources of well-being as a result of people's attempts to compensate for the negative externalities generated by the increased marketization of society.

When private goods replace the dwindling common good, defensive expenditures rise and people work harder to pay for them. This ultimately leads to a situation of growing economic affluence along with an increasing environmental and social impoverishment. The history of economic growth has a dark side where clean air, clean water, gardens, lush forests or peaceful relationships that were free for one generation become scarce and costly for the succeeding generation. The transition from an agricultural to an industrial economy has made it abundantly evident that economic growth leads to a complete decline in traditional institutions, communities and environmental degradation.

Income disparity has grown, and materialistic attitudes have taken the place of traditional values. Urban immigrants lose the safety nets offered by community relationships. The critics of industrial revolution have always pointed out how the breakdown of social ties results in a diminished sense of fulfilment in life.

Social capital in India

The Easterlin Paradox, in which rapid expansion coexists with deteriorating social capital, is also evident in the growth experiences of China and India. In the case of India, we can observe that this phenomenon is more evident in urban India than rural where the community bond is still present and acts as a social safety net. Joint families of the past offered a lot of social support but they have now been increasingly replaced by insecure nuclear families in urban India.

The sanctity of marriage is still there in India but divorces are on the rise. The new urban educated youth finds itself alone facing the battle of life. To understand SWB in India, it would be interesting to distinguish between rural and urban India. In the former, social capital would be greater, but in the latter, material things would take its place.

Conclusion

There was rapid increase in economic growth in Western countries after the Second World War but that did not lead to an increase in subjective well-being. Economic growth resulted in isolation and inequalities. This leads to the conclusion that policymakers must design policies that reduce inequalities in income and increase social capital. They must focus on quality, not the quantity of economic growth.

Aspects like environmental quality, health, tolerance and spirituality are among the prerequisites for economic progress. Economic growth by itself does not lead to increasing SWB but it is the quality of economic growth that is important. Countries must focus on this if they want to improve the happiness quotient of their citizens.

2

How GDP Failed Us

An Exploration of Measures of Growth and Happiness

"GDP is a very important measurement of everything except that which makes life worthwhile."—*Robert F Kennedy*

Is GDP an appropriate measure of development and happiness?

Almost all countries use GDP as a measure of their growth and the well-being of their citizens. In fact, most nations are obsessed with the concept of GDP and you find leaders promising higher rates of growth of GDP to their citizens. On the development index countries are ranked according to their GDP and per capita GDP, which factors in population.

In the fascinating book *The Growth Delusion,* David Pilling, a prize-winning reporter and editor with the *Financial Times* for 25 years, has been candid enough to say that GDP is an imperfect indicator of growth and development. Our policies are geared relentlessly towards increasing our standard measure of growth—gross domestic product. By this yardstick we should have been wealthier or happier than ever before. So why doesn't it feel that way? He explores how we prioritize growth maximization without stopping to think about the costs. So much of what is important to our well-being, from safe streets to sound minds, lies outside the purview of statistics. He emphasizes that GDP is morally indifferent.

Pilling is not the first person to say this but he has been absolutely forthright in his analysis, clearly bringing out the pitfalls of using GDP as a measure of economic well-being. The use of the word delusion in the title of the book is indicative of how he views rate of growth of GDP and countries putting all their energies into chasing this chimera.

The dangerous trend of rising inequality in India

The World Inequality Report 2026 (third edition), released by the World Inequality Lab and co-directed by economists such as Thomas Piketty, highlights the deepening income, wealth and gender inequalities across India and the globe.

The top 10 per cent of the people in India hold 58 per cent of the national income while the top 1 per cent hold

Figure 2.1: World Happiness Rankings 2025

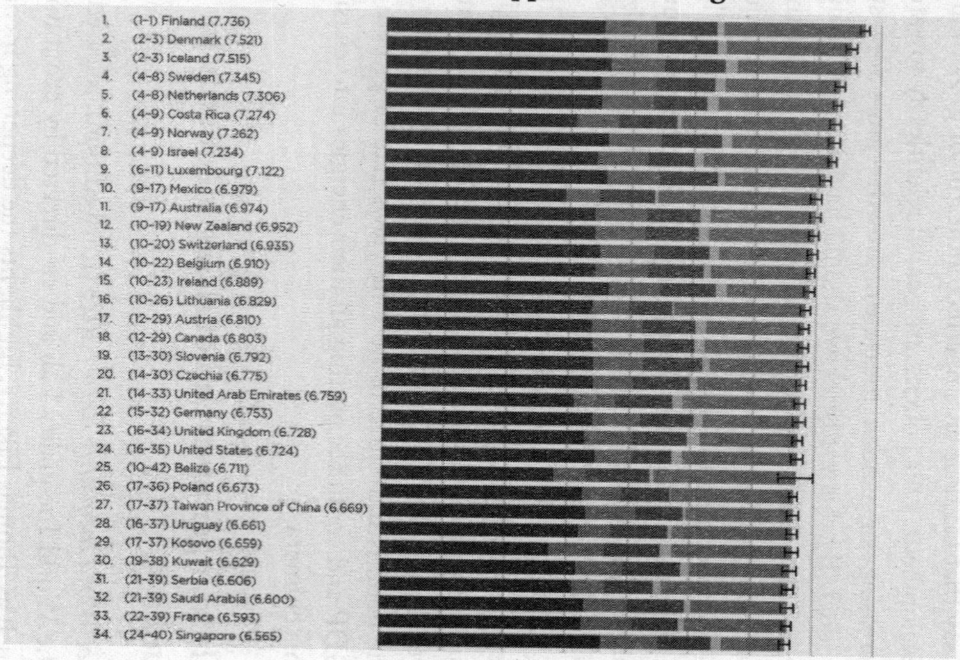

Truncated

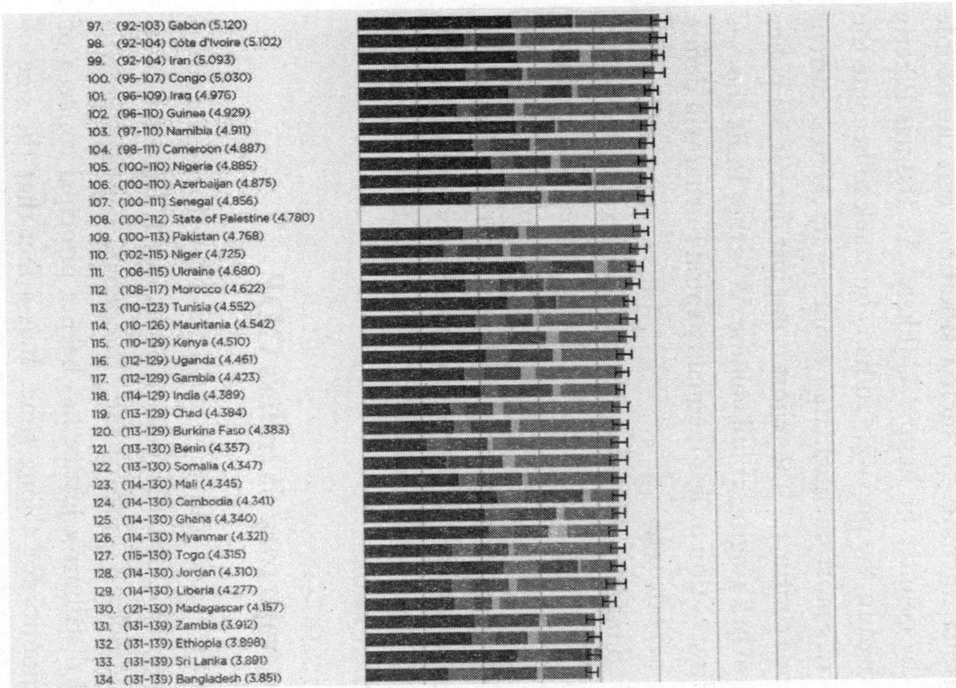

Source - https://static.poder360.com.br/2025/03/world-hapiness-report-2025.pdf

40 per cent of India's wealth, making income inequality in India among the highest in the world. In contrast, the bottom 50 per cent holds only 15 per cent of the national income. In such a situation, can the people in the country be happy? Unlikely. As Thomas Piketty warned in the preface, "India is on track to become the world's most unequal large economy by 2030 if current trends continue." The report is not just data; it is a policy alarm bell ringing at full volume. Whether India chooses redistribution or lets inequality spiral further will define the next decade.

Similarly, the richest 10 per cent account for 52 per cent of the global income while the corresponding figure for the poorest 50 per cent is only 8 per cent. The situation becomes worse when we consider the level of global wealth inequality which shows that the poor barely own any wealth (2 per cent) while the richest 10 per cent hold 76 per cent of the wealth.

The trajectory of India's GDP

India's recent budgets have put growth measured in terms of GDP as the goal to be achieved. There has been some debate on this issue. The debate between growth and distributive justice has been a principal concern of economics for a long time. It is a fact that the size of the cake matters because unless you have a high national income you will not be able to distribute it amongst the population in a way that people become better off.

For decades after independence, India's GDP grew by only 3 per cent, which has been called the Hindu rate of growth. India did not develop as fast as a number of other countries. The 1991 economic reforms ushered a period of faster economic growth but the rate of growth of employment was less than the rate of growth of GDP. High growth occurred between 2004–05 and 2010–11. The level of poverty greatly reduced during this period. However, the last few years have shown a decline in growth rates and the pandemic brought the growth rate down to negative, causing large-scale misery and unemployment. In the fourth quarter of the fiscal year 2020, the growth rate was 3.1 per cent, primarily due to the economic impact of the pandemic. However, the economy faced a severe contraction, with estimates indicating a negative growth rate of -5.83 per cent in 2021.

The Indian economy is looking up again and the government is talking about a growth rate of about 8 per cent per annum. Despite all the growth in GDP, the well-being of the people has not increased in the same proportion. *The World Happiness Report 2025* released by Wellbeing Research Centre, University of Oxford, ranks countries based on happiness levels. India ranked 118th out of 147 countries, while Finland topped the list for the eighth consecutive year (Figure 2.1). The bottom three nations are Afghanistan (147th), Sierra Leone and Lebanon. Though India's score improved from 4.054 (2021–23) to 4.389 (2022–24), it is ranked below Pakistan (109) and Nepal (92).

It demonstrates unequivocally that India is not a happy country at the moment and that, in order to make people happy, public policy should focus on their general well-being rather than just GDP growth. GDP, which is concerned with production and consumption of goods and services, is a good indicator of the level of economic activity in a country. The growth rate of GDP is significant as it does lead to a better life for people. It is more pertinent to talk of per capita GDP to assess the income level that each household is getting and the material goods and services it can consume with that income. Complete deprivation of essential goods and services leads to a poor quality of life. We cannot reject the need of material goods as they have an important bearing on the quality of life of people. It is evident that countries with greater per capita GDPs are happier than those at the lower end of the scale. Even in a country like India, states having a higher gross state domestic product and per capita income are able to provide its people a higher standard of living. It is, thus, clear that despite its limitations GDP and in particular per capita GDP do reflect the economic health of a society.

It is the real GDP that matters when we discuss GDP. This is GDP adjusted for inflation. GDP at constant prices and GDP at current prices (nominal GDP) are the two metrics that are typically used. Real GDP, often known as GDP at constant prices, is what is used to compare GDP over time. Understanding the difference between these two measures is crucial for policymakers, as decisions based on nominal GDP may not accurately reflect the economic realities faced by citizens. The GDP is calculated by using the following formula:

GDP = C + I + G + NX
C represents consumption expenditure,
I stand for investments,
G denotes government expenditure and
NX gives the figure of excess of exports over imports.

In the Indian GDP about 55 to 57 per cent is represented by consumption expenditure while 30 to 32 per cent is accounted for by investments, government expenditure is about 11 to 12 per cent while NX ranges from 1 to 2 per cent. In the post-pandemic scenario, the Indian economy is showing signs of recovery (Figure 2.2). Economists have been advocating more consumption expenditure to bring the economy back to a high growth pattern. As per some reports, India is the world's fourth-largest economy in nominal GDP terms, having overtaken Japan, which has GDP estimated at $4.18 trillion. The rise reflects a decade of rapid expansion, strong domestic demand and reforms, even as challenges like low per capita income, job creation pressures and global trade uncertainties continue to shape India's economic trajectory. India ranks behind only the US, China and Germany. This ranking is expected to be confirmed in 2026 when the final annual GDP data is released. Additionally, India is projected to surpass Germany to claim the third position within the next few years. As of the September quarter of

2025, India's GDP growth rate was 8.2 per cent, reflecting strong economic performance.

Figure 2.2: India—GDP Growth Rate (2012–2025)

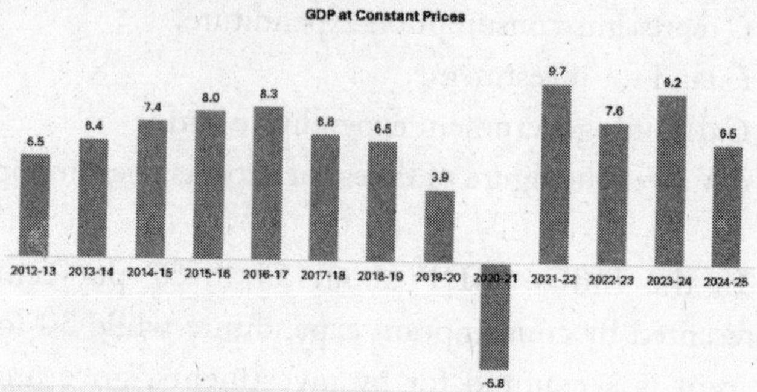

Source: Ministry of Statistics and Programme Implementation (MoSPI)

Additionally, forecasts suggest that India's GDP growth rate could reach 7.5 per cent in the fiscal year 2026–27. It is truly a remarkable achievement for India to have reached this level. However, this gives only a partial picture of the economic health of its people. A much better indicator is the per capita GDP where India is clearly still a developing economy and can in no way claim that its people have attained a sense of well-being.

Per capita GDP does indicate the level of happiness in a society even though, as we shall see later on, many important aspects of life are not a part of GDP computation. In a comparative study of countries, it is significant that India's rank in both per capita income and GNH (gross national happiness) are at the same level.

Does GDP measure up?

GDP is purely concerned with the economic aspect of a human being whether they are a producer or a consumer. However, GDP as a statistic ignores a number of key aspects of human life. Simon Kuznets recognized that national income accounts excluded valuable non-market activities, particularly the work done within households (primarily by women at the time). He understood that this omission significantly understated the true level of economic activity and well-being.

Clearly, a more holistic indicator is required. Gross national product (GNP) calculates the total value of goods and services produced by all the citizens, both in India and abroad, within a specified period. Therefore, it includes both the value of goods and services in the country, as well as the income earned by residents from overseas investments or as income earned abroad. It is calculated using the following formula:

GNP = GDP + Net income from overseas – Net income outflow abroad (income earned by foreign residents that's flowing overseas)

Robert Kennedy, who was making a bid to become the president of the United States, made one of the nicest remarks about GNP that I have ever read. Almost three months before his assassination in June 1968, he said the following at University of Kansas, "It [GNP] counts special locks for our doors and the jails for the people who break them. It counts the destruction of the redwood and the loss of our natural wonder in chaotic sprawl. It counts napalm and counts nuclear warheads and armored cars for the police to fight the riots in our cities. It counts Whitman's rifle and Speck's knife, and the television programs which glorify violence in order to sell toys to our children. Yet the gross national product does not allow for the health of our children, the quality of their education or the joy of their play. It does not include the beauty of our poetry or the strength of our marriages, the intelligence of our public debate or the integrity of our public officials. It measures neither our wit nor our courage, neither our wisdom nor our learning, neither our compassion nor our devotion to our country, it measures everything, in short, except that which makes life worthwhile. And it can tell us everything about America except why we are proud that we are Americans. If this is true here at home, so it is true elsewhere in the world."

GDP does not take into account the contribution made by homemakers who put in tremendous effort and provide their services to manage their households. If the same services are provided by a domestic help, the value of his service gets added to GDP. This way of computation of GDP does great disservice to the immense contribution made by the homemaker.

Similarly, GDP does not concern itself with morality. The GDP statistic accounts for gambling and the use of specific drugs in countries where these activities are permitted. GDP does not measure the quality of public services offered. For instance, GDP does not measure the quality of healthcare or education that is being provided to the people of a country though it would concern itself with the economic activities related to these sectors. Good governance is such a vital factor in bringing life satisfaction to people but GDP does not consider it.

As pointed out earlier, society is facing rising inequalities not merely of income but also of opportunities. Futhermore, these inequalities are widening over time, which can scarcely be said to be a happy state of affairs. GDP is a measure of growth but not of overall development. The proponents of GDP believe in the "trickledown effect" but the reality is that faster economic growth is not necessarily an indicator of the betterment of life for the millions of impoverished and underprivileged people.

Sustainable growth vs GDP growth in India

These days when we talk of economic growth we mean sustainable development which implies that we must factor in environmental issues in our computation of economic progress. There is a lot of debate about faster economic growth and its impact on environment. In 2021, the Glasgow conference on climate change once again highlighted the fact that developed countries are consuming more energy and contributing more to the generation of greenhouse gases. Ironically, these countries are exerting pressure on developing economies like India to take urgent mitigation and adaptation measures even though they are aware this could have an adverse impact on the development of these nations.

India has taken the lead by coming out with an action plan to reach net zero emissions by 2070 and to have renewable energy account for 50 per cent share of energy consumption by 2030. This would, however, require huge investments on the part of India and that is why we did not agree to completely eliminate the use of coal. Developed countries have not met their assurance of providing climate finance to the extent of 100 billion dollars per annum to developing economies to help them in their mitigation efforts. It is clear that the emission of greenhouse gases and the ensuing climate change are going to disproportionately impact the poorer countries more than the richer ones as they have much lesser resources to spend on measures for mitigation and adaptation.

In India, it is people at the lower strata of society who will suffer more. It is clear that all countries must be concerned about issues like climate change because ultimately it will impact the very existence of humanity.

Sustainable growth has also grown in importance in India, surpassing GDP growth. Roads and other infrastructure projects are required but environmental concerns of deforestation, biodiversity, wildlife preservation have to be taken into account. Moreover, large projects lead to dislocation of people which creates a huge social problem. Nowadays, an environmental impact assessment is required before most projects are started. GDP is clearly an imperfect measure of real development because it excludes the environment.

How happiness economics came into being

Going even further we find that the GDP numbers do not reflect whether people are happy. Happiness is a result of several factors which are definitely much broader and wider and perhaps more abstract than what GDP can measure. Pilling argues that the utilitarian approach of political thinker Jeremy Bentham may not provide an answer to the riddle of happiness. At its core, Bentham's utilitarianism is a theory of ethics that holds that the best action is the one that maximizes overall happiness or pleasure and minimizes overall pain or suffering. The principle he famously coined is the Greatest Happiness Principle, which suggests that the most ethical choice is the one that produces the greatest amount of happiness for the greatest number of people. This focus on happiness as the ultimate goal of ethical action marks a significant shift from previous moral systems that prioritized concepts like duty or divine command. For Bentham, happiness is a measurable, tangible thing. It is for this reason that the entire discipline of happiness economics has come into existence. Bhutan has been in the forefront of this, and the level of happiness of its citizens is currently measured by a gross national happiness index. It is clear that happiness is much more than material comfort and GDP as a measure does not consider this aspect of human life.

Per capita income as a measure of well-being

Compared to GDP, per capita income provides a far more accurate picture of the economic and social health of a nation. For instance, in terms of GDP, Uttar Pradesh has the third-largest economy in India among the states. However, it ranks third from below when comparing the states based on per capita income. As you can see both these figures give an entirely different picture. The same is true when we compare the figures across countries for GDP and per capita income.

Similar conclusions were reached by Angus Maddison in his outstanding book, *Contours of the World Economy-I-2030 AD* that compared the economy of different countries across time. For instance, the GDP of India in 1500 was 60.3 billion dollars compared to the world GDP of 248.3 billion dollars, which is almost 25 per cent of the world GDP. The corresponding figure for western Europe was 44.2 billion dollars. This would suggest that India was economically a powerful nation, but a slightly different picture appears when we look at per capita income.

The per capita income in India in 1500 was 550 dollars per annum compared to 771 dollars in western Europe and 566 dollars globally. This shows that though the Indian economy was 25 per cent of the world economy, its per capita income was marginally lower than that of the world and significantly lower than western Europe implying that standard of living of people in western Europe was higher than that in India, which does explain the future course of events.

Per capita income has also certain disadvantages; it does not take into account the inequalities of income. Also, it does not explain the degree of unemployment or poverty. Furthermore, a person's level of education and the standard of public health that are available to him determine how satisfied he is with his life, and per capita income does not account for these social variables. In the calculation of per capita income, population plays a major role as it is the denominator.

If both GDP and per capita income grow in the same proportion, we can say that economic development is taking place. However, problems may occur if population is growing at a faster rate or the population figure is high because this can skew the data. The population of India is next only to China and this explains why despite a high GDP the per capita income is on the lower side.

Despite the limitations, per capita income is nevertheless a highly useful indicator of welfare. Because of this, per capita income was one of the main characteristics when the United Nations Development Programme (UNDP) created the human development index (HDI) as a substitute indicator of development.

Dimensions of human development index

The HDI was created to emphasize that people and their capabilities should be the ultimate criteria for assessing the development of a country, not economic growth alone. The HDI was introduced in 1990 by the economist Mahbub-ul-Haq, as part of the UNDP. It was developed to measure human well-being and draws on Amartya Sen's work on human capabilities.

The HDI is a summary measure of average achievement in key dimensions of human development: a long and healthy life, being knowledgeable and having a decent standard of living. The health dimension is assessed by life expectancy at birth. The education dimension is measured by mean of years of schooling for adults aged 25 years and more and expected years of schooling for children of school-entering age. The standard of living dimension is measured by gross national income per capita.

Since 1990, the UNDP has been computing a ranking of nations using these indicators. The year 2020 was the 30th anniversary of the publication of the human development report (*HDR*). Unfortunately, India does not fare very well on this index. In 2020, India ranked 131 out of 189 countries. It clearly shows that it has a lot of work to do in terms of ensuring well-being for its people. And nothing has changed much in 2025. India is ranked 130th on the HDI with Iceland ranked at the top of the index. According to the UNDP's *Human Development Report 2025*, Norway and Switzerland occupy the second and third positions respectively while China is ranked 75th.

The first *HDR* brought out the philosophy behind this index. The main premise was that people should have a long and healthy life, they should be educated and they should have access to a decent standard of living. The report pointed out that nobody can guarantee human happiness as the choices people make are their own concern. The process of development should create a conductive environment for people individually and collectively so that they develop their full potential and have a reasonable chance of leading productive and creative lives in accordance with their needs and interests.

Public governance can focus on improving the HDI by prioritizing education, health and social justice. The pattern of governmental spending ought to reflect this. The public expenditure should be well structured so that it brings about overall improvement in the quality of life of the people.

An individual has to make additional choices regarding political freedom, personal self-respect and human rights. The political climate that guarantees these liberties and rights must be established by the state. The HDI by focusing only on the dimensions of health, education and standard of living does not bring out this aspect of human development which is also vital for improving the quality of life of the people.

Every year, *HDR*s are released in an attempt to highlight the advancements made by nations in enhancing human development elements and addressing the numerous issues that arise each year. Every *HDR* report has a special focus. The *HDR* of 2010 introduced three new measures: inequality adjusted human development index, gender inequality index and multidimensional poverty index. These metrics also highlight the fact that the well-being of a society depends on factors other than the wealth of many individuals.

There is a lot of talk about increasing inequalities in almost all countries with India being no exception. Economic growth that leads to widening of inequalities is not a true measure of development. An unequal society cannot be called a prosperous one.

Multidimensional poverty index

NITI Aayog the premier policy think tank of the Government of India has begun computing the multidimensional poverty index (MPI) for the country and states every year. India's rank in global MPI 2021 is 66 out of 109 countries, which is not a very satisfying position. NITI Aayog have deconstructed the global MPI and created a globally aligned yet customized India MPI with the objective of guiding the state to prepare comprehensive action plans for removal of poverty.

Prior to this, there were a number of indicators of poverty based on various factors, but there was a realization that per capita income or nutritional status alone did not provide a comprehensive picture and that an indicator of poverty that took into account all relevant factors was necessary. The objective of this national MPI is to compare poverty across various states, to track poverty over time and assess the level of deprivation of the multidimensional poor. The Government of India identified 29 global indices that should be monitored and analysed to lift the people of India out of poverty.

The MPI is based on the Alkire-Foster (AF) methodology which is a general framework of multidimensional poverty. The AF methodology provides an idea of not only the degree of poverty, but also a composition and distribution, making it a powerful tool of decision making. NITI Aayog has taken various dimensions to compute this index. The first of these dimensions pertains to health which comprises parameters related to nutrition, child mortality and maternal health. Each parameter has been assigned a different weight with nutrition contributing to nearly one-third of the multidimensional poverty in India. NITI Aayog has clearly identified male nutrition a major cause of poverty.

The second dimension relates to education which is represented by parameters pertaining to school attendance and year of schooling. The index measures deprivation by considering a household as being deprived if not even one member of the household aged 10 years or more has completed six years of schooling. This indicator is important because there is a clear link between education and gainful employment. The minimum qualification for any job is having passed the class 12 level. Perhaps taking 12 years of schooling might have been better but it is a fact that if a child complete six years of schooling she is likely to continue attending school.

The third dimension is that of standard of living which is represented by access of the household to basic services such as electricity, clean cooking fuel, improved and safe drinking water, improve sanitation, housing and having a bank account.

The poor are then identified on the basis of AF methodology which identifies a set of deprivation cut-offs both within and across indicators. These then lead to calculation of a deprivation score. This is followed by determining the multidimensional poor individuals in the total population which is known as the headcount ratio.

The MPI index shows the direction of policy that the government must adopt to target the poor at the federal and state levels. At the district level, it reflects the quality of implementation and indicates the steps that can be taken to improve the execution. NITI Aayog arrived at an MPI of 0.118 for India for 2021 of which 0.155 is the MPI for rural areas and 0.04 for urban areas. Kerala has the lowest percentage of multidimensional poor people (0.7 per cent), while Bihar has the largest percentage (51.9 per cent).

It is thus clear that this index is an extremely valuable tool for understanding the level of poverty and assisting the policymakers in designing policies that would improve the quality of life of the people.

Significant findings of human development reports from 2020 onwards

HDR 2020

The significant *HDR 2020 The Next Frontier: Human Development and the Anthropocene* explores the impact of the pandemic on human development. The COVID-19 pandemic had led to an alarming increase in poverty in less developed nations. The *HDR* says that the next frontier is that of human development and anthropogenic which means the age of humans. The report doubles down on the belief that people's agency and empowerment can bring about the action we need if we are to live in balance with the planet in a fairer world. It shows that we are at an unprecedented moment in history in which human activity has become a dominant force shaping the planet. Many scientists believe that for the first time, instead of the planet shaping humans, humans are knowingly shaping the planet. This is the Age of Humans. Though humanity has achieved incredible progress, we have taken the earth for granted, destabilizing the very systems upon which we rely for survival. Covid-19, which almost certainly sprang to humans from animals, offers a glimpse of our future, in which the strain on our planet mirrors the strain facing societies.

This report firmly states that we ourselves are the dominant risk to our survival. The exploitation of natural resources and destruction of the ecological environment in the thirst for greater consumption and higher material growth has led to a situation where human beings are endangering their own existence.

The poorer population is becoming more socially vulnerable as a result of this high level of ecological harm, and human society is headed towards extinction by neglecting worries about biodiversity loss and climate change. Humans must learn to respect nature and what is required is human development while taking preservation of the environment into account. This report clearly puts human development in a different perspective where the environment becomes as important as growth.

The correct model of growth should give a new meaning to a good life and not lead to rising poverty, inequality and alarming planetary change which the current model of growth is causing. The *HDR* says that though the overall size of the pie matters, the relative size of slices of the pie is perhaps more relevant.

The *HDR* 2020 lays stress on measures to mitigate and adapt to climate change, protect biodiversity and ensure well-being for all. The importance of planting more trees and creating carbon sinks cannot be overlooked. Climate change is a reality and it weakens economic progress and increases inequality. All over the world hunger is rising and migration is leading to displacement of people. Although people are at the core of progress and change agents, they are also driving the interconnected social and economic system into peril. We now need to enhance equity, foster innovation and instil a sense of environmental care. The issues relating to deforestation and gender inequality have to be addressed.

It is thus clear that though the HDI focuses on health, education and standard of living, it is not a static concept. It has been factoring the emerging challenges to human progress. As we have seen, measures pertaining to multidimensional poverty and inequality were included in 2010, and the 2020 report, which was written in the shadow of COVID-19 pandemic, highlights the critical role that ecological balance plays in ensuring human survival.

Comparing GDP and HDI

The HDI is unquestionably a more comprehensive measure of development than GDP. However, the third dimension of standard of living is measured by calculating the GDP per capita. Hence the HDI does take the GDP into account but it goes much beyond that. India should regularly prepare a *HDR* for both the nation and the states in order to properly comprehend the well-being of its people. This will help us understand the process of economic growth.

Paradoxically, many Indian states with rapid growth have human development statistics that are below average. Perhaps, it is for this reason that the political executive is wary of preparing *HDR*s and making them available to the people. However, HDI can be a highly useful tool for policymakers to prepare for the well-being of its citizens.

HDR 2021–22

The *HDR* for the period 2021–22 titled "Uncertain Times, Unsettled Lives: Shaping our Future in a World in Transformation", talks about life in unpredictable times due to COVID-19, the Russia–Ukraine conflict and other ecological disasters. The report is of the view that uncertainty is increasing every day and unsettling human lives. Destabilizing global pressures, rising inequality and profound societal changes have come together to establish the new normal.

As a consequence of the pandemic, people have been feeling more insecure about their lives. A lot of lives were lost and there has been highly unequal access to vaccines. There was a breakdown of trust and cooperation among and within nations. The *HDR* challenged the conventional notions of progress. Human growth is "a means to a path forward in uncertain times reminding us that people in all our complexity, our diversity, our creativity are the real wealth of nations." Throughout history, humans have encountered uncertainty, and they have learned ways to deal with it. According to the report, the three volatile crosscurrents are:

- The dangerous planetary change of the Anthropocene.
- The pursuit of sweeping societal transformations on par with the Industrial Revolution.
- The vagaries and vacillations of polarized societies

Ironically, the report claims that although we have greater capacity to make decisions about the future, we do not have more influence over it. Climate change and disruptive technological advances are influencing future outcome in a manner human beings are unable to comprehend fully or keep pace with. According to the HDI's statistical research, there has been a deterioration for the past two years, to the point that the advances from the previous five years have been negated. However, there is no need to be unnecessarily pessimistic and there is still hope. Investment, insurance and innovation will help people handle the new uncertainty.

Investment is required in areas from renewable energy to preparedness for pandemic and natural calamities. Insurance is about social protection and the potential benefits of investing in health and education. In terms of technology, the economy and culture, innovation is crucial. We have to use technology to provide creative solutions to human society and it should augment the capacity of labour rather than displace it.

Human development has been negatively impacted by unequal availability of vaccines in low-income countries, particularly in Africa. As of 27 July 2022, only 21 per cent of people in low-income countries had received at least one dose of vaccinations. Inequalities in education and women's position have been exacerbated by this vaccination disparity.

Climate change is a reality and our response to this is not fast enough to prevent less developed countries from experiencing its impact and becoming even more impoverished and underdeveloped. Ecosystems are under great stress and there is an increase in conflicts due to social imbalance. Environmental conflicts are on the rise and with the inequalities of political and economic power they are becoming more a matter of concern. The report says that there is a large degree of political polarization and many people are getting alienated from political systems.

The *HDR 2022* describes technology as a double-edged sword and acknowledges its disruptive influence on our lives. Digitization is the call of the day and social media has taken over. The use of new technological tools for data analysis is growing. While new employment opportunities are being created, some people are losing their positions. The ability of human society to use technology in a meaningful and intentional way is the answer to the problem. The benefits of technology should outweigh the drawbacks.

The *HDR* laments that despite the awareness of the continuous mounting pressure of environmental distress leading to climate change, countries are not responding in the desired manner. The more developed countries are responsible for a higher degree of greenhouse gas emissions but they are not forthcoming enough to take accountability and take appropriate action. For less developed countries, the dilemma is the trade-off between growth and environmental protection.

This report emphasizes the point made in the *HDR 2019* that one needs to go beyond averages and examine the variations in the development and capabilities in various countries. The purpose of human existence is to enable individuals to realize their full potential by enhancing their capacities, which encompass not only well-being, accomplishments but also agency and freedom.

A disturbing trend and challenges for the future

A disturbing conclusion of the *HDR* is that there was a decline in HDI across all countries in 2020–21. This could be largely due to the impact of the pandemic. Accordingly, the report believes that increased ambiguity can have a negative impact on people's mental health by making them feel more anxious and insecure. Mental disorder can lead to other health challenges and reduce productivity. School attendance and learning are also likely to be negatively impacted. All countries have to work together to address the challenges thrown up by the new uncertainties.

The report strikes a positive note by saying that some good can also emerge from the situation. For instance, artificial intelligence (AI) can enhance the capacity of labour and make it more productive. This could lead to newer and better paid jobs. Also, people are learning to respond more creatively to the uncertainties.

The *HDR* candidly says that we have to learn how to deal with today's difficulties through trial and error. We have to try and set the direction though we are not sure of the outcome. However, human society is now better equipped with tools to shape their lives. The report is optimistic and states that though the future maybe uncertain there will be more "promise than peril".

The *HDR* finds that negative views about the world and the future have escalated to previously unheard-of levels. Perceived insecurity is rising even in some nations with extremely high HDI. The number of people reporting negative emotions of stress, sadness, anger and worry has been on the rise with this being more visible in women, people with lesser education and people who are underemployed or unemployed. The global effort to reduce extreme poverty has been hampered by the COVID-19 epidemic. We witnessed this in India also where a study calculated that 23 million people were pushed into poverty due to the pandemic.

The situation would be similar in many of the world's less developed countries. The unfortunate aspect of the current situation is that people and nations with lesser levels of development are more vulnerable to risks to human life. The report is hopeful that people will respond by taking action to create a more safe and just world. The responsibility falls more heavily on those who are better off and have the power to influence the course of things.

For example, decisions made today by governments and individuals will determine the potential future state of climate change. The report sounds a note of caution by saying that for the first time in human history, anthropogenic existential threats outweigh those arising from natural hazards. The report states that humans have always had the capacity to harm each other but today they have reached a level where a large number of global populations faces extinction.

Another challenge before nations is that of energy transition from fossil fuels towards more renewable energy and at a lower cost. In the November 2024 international conference on climate change in Baku, Azerbaijan, this aspect was discussed in great depths and countries promised to make themselves net zero by a certain date. Even India has made a commitment to do away with fossil fuels by 2070. However, this is not going to be easy as renewable energy requires technology related to battery storage and development of sustainable and cost-efficient long-duration energy storage system which will take some time to come.

Nevertheless, this is feasible since every country has begun to take steps towards energy transition by creating legislation and receiving backing from social movements. This energy transformation demands minerals and materials that add to planetary pressures.

Rising mental distress

The *HDR* is of the view that mental distress is an obstacle to human development because unsettled minds cannot create a better world. Due to mental health issues people are unable to live the life they want to and, in particular, the future of children suffers the most. Children suffer from poor education achievements and the society faces issues of low productivity at work, poverty, poor health, shorter life and higher death rate. Lack of mental well-being adversely influences a person's ability to contribute to social and economic development. Such individuals are not able to make a good living or lead long healthy lives, resulting in a low sense of well-being.

In uncertain times, like the pandemic, the level of mental distress in the society goes up significantly. Economic insecurity aggravates mental distress. Additionally, children's emotional and physical health, brain and body development, and cognitive functioning can all get negatively impacted by living in impoverished environments, which can also lower their aspirations and goals. The *HDR* even goes so far as to claim that this high level of uncertainty exposes certain individuals to the evil of human trafficking. All this leads to greater economic inequality and lower level of happiness.

Rising social polarization and insecurity

According to the *HDR*, we are aware of our problems and also have the tools to address them but we are failing to act in trying to understand why this is happening. Uncertainty leads to challenges like political extremism which is on the rise. And the abundance of hyper information is creating divisions in society. The space for public deliberation is shrinking at a time when it is required the most. Uncertainty causes people to live uneasy and insecure lives, which can exacerbate division and affect the social choice process. The report tries to understand how it is difficult to act individually and collectively in the face of uncertainty.

To track human insecurity, the report uses an index of perceived human insecurity which it computes for 77 countries and territories covering about 80 per cent of global population. This index addresses instability arising from conflict-related insecurity, socio-economic insecurity, and insecurity at the personal and community levels. Human insecurity directly restricts human agency and leads to lower level of trust between people. The current environment in which countries are facing common challenges requires a high level of cooperation between various groups. Political extremism, or the unwavering pursuit of one objective over another, is also associated with increased human insecurity. The combination of high level of uncertainty and high inequality often leads to a situation which favours emergence of authoritarian leaders who are less likely to foster intra-group and inter-group cooperation.

Interestingly, the report concludes that increased polarization bears a close relation to levels of human well-being, including greater economic prosperity, uptake of new technology and improvements in health, education and gender equality. This suggests that what we call development may not deliver for people as expected. The *HDR* uses a positive peace index (PPI) measuring the positive peace of 163 countries. Positive peace is defined as the attitude, institutions and structures that create and sustain peaceful societies. India's rank is 115th out of 163 countries on this index. See Figure 2.3 for more details.

The conclusion is that advancements in the structures domain rather than the attitudes domain have been responsible for the PPI's improvement over the previous 10 years. This is the paradox of growing social polarization and economic advancement.

Despite considerable progress, societies have become less harmonious and more factionalized and intolerant. Considerable advancement in digital technology has taken place providing new ways to groups to interact but they have been disruptive of the existing social networks. The report finds that advances in digital communication risk destabilizing societies.

Figure 2.3: Gobal Peace Index

Source: Institute for Economics & Peace

Severe polarization can make people oblivious of the fact that there are common grounds and strategies that can be formulated where everybody gains. Life is not a zero-sum game. Polarization also adversely impacts international cooperation. According to data from nations with extremely high human development indices, support for democracy is under pressure. This is closely correlated with the degree of insecurity, and those who are insecure are less likely than those who feel secure to value democracy.

Advance of modern technology

The pandemic has been the main cause for this atmosphere of uncertainty. However, it is not as if everything is dismal. This uncertainty has also presented new opportunities that go beyond conventional thinking and enable one to re-imagine the future. Countries responded to the pandemic by coming up with new vaccines and also innovative physical and monetary interventions. Rapidly evolving technologies such as AI and synthetic biology could usher in a new era of prosperity for the people and the planet, and steer the world towards greater human development.

The new technological advances are the engines that will fuel future economic growth like they have done in the past. These advances shall create a lot of disruption and society will have to develop social systems to adjust to these changes so that they can fulfil the potential of advancing human development. Technological changes affect human capabilities in multiple ways. They not only expand our ability to do more things but also affect our social context and people's ability to make choices regarding their goals. Innovation is more than just invention; it is linked to agency, which employs the ability of people to act on their values, ideas and priorities.

The report is clear that new technologies have the potential of advancing human capabilities and progress but it also cautions that the rapid pace of technological changes may create new challenges like misuse and thorny political and ethical issues and other intended consequences. It is for these reason that human societies will have to carefully navigate the route for future development. The impact of technology would also be unequal as became evident during the pandemic and as substantiated by the varying rate of vaccination in different countries

The access and availability of vaccines were grossly unequal across countries during the pandemic. Moreover, there was a decline in human index value between 2020 and 2021 because of it but this decline was also grossly unequal with low HDI countries suffering the maximum. The response to the pandemic has also shown that people-centric policies substantially enhance human well-being. Most countries like the US, the UK, Germany, Japan and India extended monetary support and health measures during the pandemic in the form of vaccines medical equipment and stimulus packages. The pandemic disrupted the world but it is now over and things are returning to normal but there are a lot of lessons that the pandemic has taught. The World Health Organization declared the COVID-19 pandemic over on 5 May 2023.

The response to the crises has shown that the world can be more just and resilient. It has also shown that it is possible to reorient the relationship between government and people and this can bring about significant improvement in the lives of the people. The monetary support and provision of healthcare facilities created a sense of security among citizens.

The path to transformation

Finally, the report tries to indicate the paths of transformations which will help navigate the uncertainty to expand human development. The focus should be on the three I's—investment, insurance and innovation—which will together stimulate human development and enable the people and the planet to flourish. According to the report, culture has a big role to play and it identifies three enablers of cultural change—education to cultivate evolving values, social recognition to legitimize them, and representation to protect their inclusivity and translate them into policies.

Investment in the capabilities of the people would be required to enable progress. To allow these changes to take place, culture has a vital role to play. Encouraging education will allow people to shape their own future. The next step is recognition of human rights and respect for people's identity and values that would help build hope in society and representation to give voice to the marginalized.

The report is candid in admitting that there cannot be one set of policy recommendation to suit every country but these ideas can be used as a compass to navigate.

Four principles—systemic thinking, transparency, social inclusion and subsidiarity—would have to constitute the foundation of governance in order to achieve systemic and transformative change. Governance would have to be transparent and inclusive.

This *HDR* is all about how human society can respond to uncertain times. This would require unlocking of the human potential to let flexibility, creativity, solidarity and inclusion guide the future. Despite the uncertainty the *HDR* feels that the future promises to be better if the right kinds of choices are made.

HDR 2023–2024

The *HDR 2023-2024 Breaking the Gridlock: Reimagining Cooperation in a Polarized World*, addresses the global challenges of uneven development progress, intensifying inequality and escalating political polarization. The HDI value might have been greater if the epidemic had not happened. In fact, before the crisis brought about by the pandemic, the world was on track to meet the SDG deadlines by 2030 and also attain a considerably higher HDI value.

The Sustainable Development Goals (SDGs) are a set of 17 goals established by the UN in 2015 as part of the 2030 Agenda for Sustainable Development. The goals include:

- No poverty
- Zero hunger
- Quality education

- Good health and well-being
- Gender equality
- Clean water and sanitation
- Affordable and clean energy
- Decent work and economic growth
- Industry, innovation and infrastructure
- Reduced inequality
- Sustainable cities and communities
- Responsible consumption and production
- Climate action
- Conserve life below water
- Protect life on land
- Peace, justice and strong institutions
- Partnerships for the goals

These goals are interconnected and are designed to be achieved by 2030 to ensure a sustainable future for all.

However, the *HDR* indicates that richer countries are recovering from the effects of the pandemic much faster than the poorer countries. The poorest are struggling. All member countries of the Organization for Cooperation on Economic Development (OECD) have gone beyond their 2019 HDI levels whereas the same is not true for the countries at the bottom of the development pyramid. This creates a dangerous situation of increasing the inequality between nations which the authors of the report have called "gridlock", which has the potential to lead to political polarization. Political polarization results in legislative gridlock and policymaking processes. It leads to governmental dysfunction and a decline in trust in democratic processes and institutions. This further intensifies partisanship, fosters media fragmentation and undermines democratic norms such as the rule of law and the independence of the judiciary. This issue needs to be urgently tackled at the global level because rising inequality and political polarization lead to a reduction in the level of happiness of the people.

The *HDR* claims a reduction in inequalities across the world in the last 20 years, but this has been reversed. It makes the startling observation that 40 per cent of global trade in goods and services is concentrated in 3 or 4 countries. In 2021, the market capitalization of each of the three largest technology companies—Apple, Microsoft and Google—surpassed the GDP of more than 90 per cent of the countries that year. The report states that in order to address our shared and existential challenges and ensure people's aspirations are met, we must make use of both our interdependence and our capabilities.

Achim Steiner, the then administrator of UNDP, further adds, "The gridlock carries a significant human toll. The failure of collective action to advance action on climate change, digitalization, poverty and inequality not only hinders human development but also worsens polarization and further erodes trust in people and institutions worldwide."

The report suggests four areas for immediate action:

1. *Planetary public goods for climate stability* as we confront the unprecedented challenges of the Anthropocene Age.

2. *Digital global public goods for greater equity* in harnessing new technologies for equitable human development.
3. *New and expanded financial mechanisms*, including a novel track in international cooperation that complements humanitarian assistance and traditional development aid to low-income countries.
4. *Dialing down political polarization* through new governance approaches focused on enhancing people's voices in deliberation and tackling misinformation.

India has also seen a rise in inequality and its HDI values have decreased by 31.1 per cent as a result of this. India's HDI score has shown an improvement after a drop in 2021 from a value of 0.633 to 0.644 in 2022. This puts the nation in the 134th place out of 193, classifying it as a medium human development country. Between 1990 and 2022, India has shown improvement in its HDI score by 48.4 per cent going up from 0.434 in 1990 to 0.644 in 2022. In 2022, India was ranked 108th out of 166 nations in the gender inequality index (GII), which analyses gender inequality in three dimensions: labour market, empowerment and reproductive health. Significantly, India's GII value of 0.437 is better than the global average of 0.462. However, India has one of the worst gender disparities in the labour force participation rate—a 47.8 per cent discrepancy between women at 28.3 per cent and men at 76.1 per cent.

India has shown remarkable progress in human development since 1990 with life expectancy at birth having risen by 9.1 years, expected years of schooling having increased by 4.6 years and mean years of schooling have grown by 3.8 years. There is, of course, considerable room for improvement to create a more equitable and brighter future for all.

The report is concerned with the increasing polarization at the political level that is taking place within countries and at the global level. It argues for diversity and debate but is wary of the negative effects of polarization. The report is of the view that polarization poisons everything it touches and impedes international cooperation. It also self-destructs. The *HDR* 2023–24 also brings out the democracy paradox whereby there is unwavering support for democracy in the world but increasing support for leaders who may undermine it. It calls for institutions to become people-centric. The *HDR* advocates interdependence between nations in an atmosphere of peace to bring about human development for all. This is the recipe for happiness that emerges from the *HDR*.

HDR 2025

The 2025 HDR A Matter of Choice: People and Possibilities in the Age of AI highlights the crucial role of human decision-making in harnessing AI for global development. Unlike previous reports that focus solely on AI's capabilities, this report emphasizes the potential for choices to open new pathways for human progress parallel to AI advancements. The report champions the power of imagination to reshape economies and societies, ensuring equitable development in an AI-influenced world.

The *HDR 2025* says that AI will reshape human development and that human choices and not technology alone will determine whether AI contributes to inclusive development. It cautions that AI should be used to enhance human capabilities and not to replace them or deepen inequalities. The core insight of the report is that the future impact of AI would depend to a large extent on the policy decisions that we take and regulatory frameworks that we formulate to improve the dissemination of the benefits of artificial intelligence. The report also shows concern that the progress in HDI has shown a marked decline in most countries.

By and large, the global trends in HDI show that the Nordic countries—Norway, Denmark, Sweden and Finland—are the world leaders in HDI and rank in the top 10. Norway has been at the top position for several years. The explanation is that these nations have a strong social security system, good state intervention in health and education, and high per capita income. The countries at the bottom of the list are Niger, Eritrea, Chad and Burundi. India has become a middle-level country as far as HDI is concerned. Indian policymakers must focus on the three dimensions of HDI in order to move higher in the list and make their citizens happier. As of 2025, India ranked 130 out of 193 countries in the HDI, reflecting progress in life expectancy, education and income, but also highlighting ongoing challenges such as gender and income inequality.

Is HDI a better measure of human happiness than GDP?

The HDI is a superior measure of human welfare and happiness because it puts the individual at the centre of the index. The per capita income dimension gives the standard of living or quality of life. The other two parameters relate to health and education which are vital for the well-being of people. However, it is not a perfect index as it talks about education and health but does not give any indication about the quality of health and education, which is crucial if we want to develop the human capital and make them happy. It also does not take into account the level of unemployment in a country which can be a crucial determinant of the level of happiness.

"People are the real wealth of a nation," Haq wrote in the opening lines of the first report in 1990. "The basic objective of development is to create an enabling environment for people to enjoy long, healthy and creative lives. This may appear to be a simple truth. But it is often forgotten in the immediate concern with the accumulation of commodities and financial wealth."

The HDI score of any country, including India, can improve if they give prominence to issues related to health, education and social justice. Each *HDR* has selected an area for special focus, like the *HDR* 2010 focused on inequality and *HDR* 2020 on COVID-19 and its impact on poverty, and the emphasis on the three dimensions.

The HDI also has certain weaknesses. Many people are critical of the index on the ground that it takes GDP per capita into account but does not give any indication of the income distribution. For instance, the per capita income of India ignores the huge inequalities of income and also regional differences. A country as vast as India has to take into account the differences in the per capita income of the southern and the northern states before they formulate any public policy. India is so diverse that policymakers have to be conscious of the fact that one policy cannot apply to the entire country.

Regional differences have to be taken into account because we want the entire nation to develop and be happy and not just a few parts of it. GDP does not show how income is spent by the government and it is a fact that some countries spend more on military than healthcare. There are in India and in other countries a large number of people living in extreme poverty but the HDI is not able to capture this.

The HDI is also flawed because it averages out the score in the three dimensions though some factors may be more important than others particularly when you want to relate HDI with happiness. Regarding knowledge also, many critics say that it takes into account what children learn at school and ignores the learning that is imparted by the family at home. Longevity can also be distorted as the life expectancy of a person does not consider how healthy is the life that person has led. For example, the HDI would assign a higher value to a person aged 90 years but who has suffered serious illnesses in the last 30 years of his life than to a person who lived for 70 years but led a very healthy life.

Furthermore, many nations lack religious freedom despite having rapidly expanding economies and highly advanced health and education systems. There is censorship on media and internet. These nations, where the government meddles in every aspect of citizens' lives, cannot be considered truly developed, and their citizens would undoubtedly be unhappy. HDI also suffers from the fact that the data from some developing countries may not be very accurate or reliable. The three measures chosen appear to many as being arbitrary and more factors need to be evaluated.

Thus, HDI is a better indicator of human development and happiness than GDP, but it is not a perfect measure. While policymakers must concentrate on the HDI, they must also advance to measures such as SDG and GNH in order to make people happy. While the HDI focuses on core dimensions of human development through quantifiable indicators, GNH takes a more comprehensive approach by considering psychological well-being and cultural preservation alongside material prosperity.

3

Gross National Happiness Index

Rethinking What a Healthy Economy Means

"If with a pure mind, one speaks or acts, happiness will follow like a shadow that never departs."— Buddha

How gross national happiness emerged as an important measure of human welfare

Our discussion in the earlier chapter clearly brings out the fact that GDP is an inadequate measure of economic development and human welfare. There have been various alternatives suggested to create a holistic index which captures all aspects of development, gross national happiness (GNH) being one of them. The mountain country of Bhutan and its visionary king Jigme Singye

Wangchuck decided to use GNH as the goal to aspire for in order to ensure sustainable development of the country by giving importance not only to economic factors, but also non-economic factors which have a significant bearing on the sense of well-being of the individual and the society. The concept of GNH emerged in the 1970s when King Wangchuck famously declared,"Gross national happiness is more important than gross national product."

This was not just a catchy slogan; it represented a fundamental philosophical shift in how a nation should measure its success. The young king, who ascended to the throne at just 16, recognized that economic development alone could not guarantee the well-being of his people.

Unlike many developing nations that pursued rapid industrialization and economic growth at any cost, Bhutan chose a different path. The country's approach was deeply rooted in Buddhist philosophy, which emphasizes the interdependence of all beings and the pursuit of happiness through spiritual and material balance. This philosophical foundation became the cornerstone of Bhutan's unique development model, setting it apart from its neighbours and the broader international community.

The four pillars of gross national happiness

The GNH framework rests on four fundamental pillars that guide all policy decisions and development initiatives in Bhutan. Each pillar represents a crucial aspect of human well-being and societal progress. They include:

1. Promotion of sustainable development
2. Preservation of cultural values
3. Conservation of natural environment
4. Establishment of good governance

Unlike GDP, which is relatively straightforward to calculate, measuring happiness presents unique challenges. Bhutan has developed a sophisticated methodology that uses 33 indicators across nine domains to assess the nation's well-being.

Measuring happiness the GNH index way

The GNH index uses a multidimensional approach, collecting data through comprehensive surveys conducted every five years. Respondents answer questions about their satisfaction with various aspects of life, from their health and education to their sense of community belonging and cultural identity. The data is then analysed to produce both individual and collective happiness scores.

Bhutan uses GNH as an index to shape social and economic policies and act as a measurement tool to assess changes in the level of well-being. This index is a comprehensive measure of the level of health, education, quality of life and even psychological well-being. The government of Bhutan realized that happiness is both an internal and external phenomena which requires a holistic index to measure. This methodology recognizes that happiness is subjective and multifaceted, requiring a more nuanced approach than simple economic indicators. The index provides policymakers with detailed insights into which areas need attention and how different policies might impact overall well-being.

The GNH index has identified the following nine important domains:

1. *Psychological well-being*: Measures happiness, satisfaction and emotional well-being.
2. *Health*: Assesses physical and mental health.
3. *Time use*: Examines how people allocate their time between work, leisure and other activities.
4. *Education*: Evaluates access to and quality of education.
5. *Cultural diversity and resilience*: Measures the preservation and promotion of cultural heritage.
6. *Good governance*: Assesses the quality of governance, including factors like corruption and transparency.
7. *Community vitality*: Evaluates the strength and cohesion of communities.
8. *Ecological diversity and resilience*: Measures the health and sustainability of the natural environment.
9. *Living standards*: Assesses material well-being, including income and access to basic necessities.

These domains provide a comprehensive framework for measuring well-being and are used to inform policy decisions. Each one of these domains is further divided into indicators. There are a total of 33 indicators in these domains.

This index identifies four groups of people:

1. Unhappy
2. Narrowly happy
3. Extensively happy and
4. Deeply happy

This approach benchmarks the current position regarding these four groups of people and then focuses on how policies can lead to an increase in their level of happiness.

The 2011 UN resolution on happiness

Bhutan's GNH philosophy has gained significant international attention and recognition. The UN has acknowledged the importance of happiness and well-being in development, partly influenced by Bhutan's advocacy.

In 2011, the UN unanimously adopted a General Assembly resolution introduced by Bhutan with support from 68 member countries calling for a holistic approach to development aimed at promoting sustainable happiness and well-being. This built on Bhutan's concept of the GNH index. Several countries and regions have begun incorporating well-being measures into their policy frameworks. For example, Sikkim has expressed interest in adopting GNH principles, while countries like Costa Rica have developed their own happiness indices. The European Union has also started measuring well-being alongside economic indicators in its policy assessments. As of 2025, no country has officially acknowledged GNH as a primary development indicator. The concept of GNH is primarily associated with Bhutan, where it has been adopted as a holistic approach to development, emphasizing non-economic aspects of well-being.

International organizations, including the World Bank and the OECD, have begun recognizing the limitations of purely economic measures of progress and are exploring alternative indicators that include social and environmental factors.

In each of the nine domains mentioned earlier there are two to four indicators some of which are objective indicators and are given higher weight while the subjective and self-reported indicators are assigned much lesser weight. The idea is to give greater importance to measurable indicators.

The 2011 GNH index identifies happiness as comprising sufficient achievement in 66 per cent of the weighted indicators. Such people would be considered as being extensively happy or deeply happy. People who have achieved sufficiency in less than 50 per cent are unhappy while those in the range of 50 to 65 per cent are called narrowly happy.

The goal of public policy is to move people out of the unhappy and narrowly happy states to the extensively and deeply happy level. The index can be broken down by population groups or by geographical areas or other factors like education to enable the policymaker to focus on the deficient areas so that increasing number of people move towards a happier state of life.

In Bhutan, the GNH index has been used for policymaking. It reviews the impact of various policies on the index and also tracks the level of improvement over time. The ideal situation is that every policy has to be tested against the lens of the GNH index before formulation and implementation. The same applies to the process of screening government projects in nearly 20 project areas including agriculture, forestry, trade and manufacturing, media and information. The whole idea is that all government projects and policies have to work together to maximize GNH. For the purpose of policy screening, the following 26 criteria of GNH are used:

1. Equity
2. Economic security
3. Material well-being
4. Engagement in productive activities
5. Decision-making opportunity
6. Corruption
7. Judiciary efficiency
8. Judiciary access
9. Rights
10. Gender equality
11. Information
12. Learning
13. Health
14. Water pollution
15. Air pollution

16. Land degradation
17. Conservation of plants
18. Conservation of animals
19. Social support
20. Family
21. Nature
22. Recreation
23. Culture
24. Values
25. Spiritual pursuits
26. Stress

Each of these criteria is weighted on a 4-point scale ranging from 1 to 4. After a project or policy has been screened by the Gross National Happiness Commission (GNHC) the issue is put up before the cabinet for final approval.

It is necessary to point out that the Bhutanese concept of happiness is based on the Buddhist understanding of life and is a much broader concept than happiness as it is understood in the West. The GNH in Bhutan covers a whole range of human well-being like living standards, health, education, psychological well-being, culture, community vitality and environmental diversity.

King Jigme Khesar Namgyel Wangchuck has expressed the vision in a concise manner by saying, "Today, GNH has come to mean so many things to so many people but to me, it signifies simply—development with values. Thus for my nation, today GNH is the bridge between the fundamental values of kindness, equality and humanity and the necessary pursuit of economic growth."

How Bhutan went about implementing policy with a focus on GNH

The Government of Bhutan constituted the GNHC to implement GNH in Bhutan. The importance of the commission can be gauged from the fact that the Prime Minister of Bhutan is the chairperson of this commission and the secretary of various ministries are members. This commission conceives a five-year plan for the nation to improve its level of happiness and is also tasked with the implementation of these plans and resultant policies. The Government of Bhutan conducted its first GNH survey in 2008, followed by another one in 2010 and then 2015. This survey covers all 20 districts of Bhutan and was based on questionnaires.

Each of these districts of Bhutan has a district administration with a district chief executive known as *dzongdag*. The district government board is known as Dzongkhag Tshogdu. The district administration carries out the decisions of the district government board. However, the civil servants in the districts are also responsible to their parent ministry in the central government. This is a situation of dual control which does create some administrative issues. The districts are further divided into *gewogs* which are the lowest layer of local body administration managed by an elected chairperson and members with civil servants as non-voting observers. These civil servants also report to their seniors at the district level and these multiple accountabilities do impact the realization of GNH outcomes.

In 2022, the GNHC was officially dissolved as part of the Royal Civil Service Commission's reorganization of civil service agencies.

GNH and Bhutan's success story

The Bhutan GNH index measures societal progress in a similar manner as the OECD's better life index and social progress index. However, the Bhutan index includes religious components. The data generated by GNH is used to compare happiness between different groups of people and on different parameters. Incidentally in 2012, the Prime Minister of Bhutan Jigme Thinley met with the secretary general of the UN Ban Ki-moon and defined a new economic paradigm to encourage the spread of Bhutan's GNH philosophy. This high-level meeting led to the release of the first world happiness report (*WHR*) on 1 April 2012. According to the *WHR 2019*, Bhutan is ranked 95th out of 156 countries on the GNH index.

Following this, the UN General Assembly proclaimed 20 March as the International Day of Happiness in 2013, recognizing the relevance of happiness and well-being as universal goals and aspirations in public policy. It is interesting to note that the vision of the government as one whose main purpose is to provide happiness to its people was part of the 1729 legal Code of Bhutan.

Bhutan's 2010 GNH poll included questions about both immediate and long-term emotions. Although people are conscious of their current emotions, they frequently struggle to recall the experiences that are associated with them in the past. Additionally, people tend to remember the strength of feelings more than their frequency, which might lead to biased answers. Despite these drawbacks, the surveys carried out by the Bhutanese government did provide a standard by which the effects of upcoming initiatives could be evaluated.

The GNH is a measure of the well-being of the people though the constituents of this well-being would vary between different cultures and over different time periods. However, the broad areas of GNH are likely to remain the same. The GNH index attempts to measure both subjective as well as objective aspects of well-being. In fact, of the 33 indicators used, 24 are qualitative and 9 are quantitative. To compute the index it is important to assign the right kind of weights to each indicator. The nine domains of GNH are equally weighted to reflect equal importance to each domain in happiness. These domains broadly reflect the purposes of governance.

The 33 indicators used in constructing the GNH index consist of:

1. Five life satisfactions
2. Five negative emotions

3. Five positive emotions—emotional balance index
4. Four activities composing spirituality index
5. Self-reported health status
6. Healthy days in a month
7. Long-term disability index
8. Mental health
9. Literacy
10. Educational qualification
11. Knowledge index
12. Index of five values
13. Mother tongue proficiency
14. Thirteen artisan skills—making up the artisan skill index
15. Participation in cultural and communities activities
16. Way of harmony (interpersonal etiquette and courtesy)
17. 8-hour limit of working hours
18. 8 hours of minimum sleep
19. 2 activities of political participation index
20. Fundamental rights index
21. 7 core activities of government performance index
22. 4 basic government service delivery index
23. 3 activities of social support index
24. 2 activities of community vitality index
25. Good family index
26. Victimization index
27. Pollution index
28. Environmental responsibility attitude
29. Wildlife depredation index
30. Public transport accessibility

31. Household income
32. Ownership of appliances, life stock, land composing assets index
33. Housing quality index

It is clear from the above indicators that they are extremely comprehensive and cover almost all aspects of human life though quantification of these could be a difficult task.

It is necessary to mention that the role of the private sector and rural farmers is not fully captured in the GNH index. This is an anomaly as the private sector contributes to almost half the GDP and is engaged in important activities like retailing, manufacturing, banking, insurance, construction, transport and tourism. It is felt by experts that the private sector has not been fully guided towards GNH. Now that Bhutan is now opening up to foreign direct investment and becoming more business friendly, the role of the private sector would get integrated with the computation of GNH.

Multilateral or bilateral development partners who provide grants and soft loans for the capital expenditure of Bhutan also have a critical role to play in the development of the nation. They generally support Bhutan with regard to its GNH vision and government priorities. Yet each development partner has its own interests.

Bhutan's development has now successfully entered its 60th year. A lot of success achieved by the country can be attributed to their focus on gross national happiness. Bhutan has made significant strides in reducing poverty, with rates dropping from 28 per cent in 2017 to 11.6 per cent in 2022, according to a new report by the World Bank. The report attributes this progress to economic growth, increased agricultural productivity, labour market changes, COVID-19 relief efforts and remittances.

It is also being found that enrolment in both primary and secondary education has significantly increased with the former going up by 30 per cent between 2007 and 2017. Infrastructure has also developed and now 91 per cent of the Bhutanese population lives within one-hour distance to a health facility compared to 73 per cent in 2007. The farm road network has increased from 1,700 km to 11,200 km between 2008 and 2017.

It is, however, debatable whether GNH being used as a measure of development has been responsible for this growth. Some experts argue that even before the use of GNH by Bhutan, the country had been taking steps in the direction of improving education and health, and the current trend is merely a continuation of good public policy. However, it cannot be denied that education and health are priority items in the GNH index and though Bhutan is a developing country and has paucity of resources they have being utilizing their limited means wisely and both education and healthcare are free for citizens of Bhutan.

We have already seen that GNH is fully concerned with preservation of the environment. Bhutan has a rich forest cover which comprises 72 per cent of its total area. The nation takes great pride in the fact that it is not only a carbon neutral state but, perhaps, one of the only countries which is carbon negative. This achievement was much appreciated in the conference on climate change in Paris in December 2015. Hydro power is the main source of energy in Bhutan in which it has become self-sufficient and is in a position to export it also. This makes it clear that the GNH index consciously focuses on sustainable development and on countering and mitigating the adverse impact of climate change which threatens the very foundation of human existence.

Challenges of GNH as a measure for growth

While GNH has gained international acclaim, it has also faced criticism and challenges. Some economists argue that without strong economic growth, it is difficult to provide the resources necessary for health, education and other well-being indicators. Critics point out that Bhutan still faces poverty and unemployment challenges, suggesting that economic development should not be entirely subordinated to other goals. There are also concerns about the subjective nature of happiness measurement and whether it can provide reliable guidance for policy decisions. Some argue that the GNH approach might work in a small, relatively homogeneous society like Bhutan but could be difficult to implement in larger, more diverse countries. Additionally, balancing tradition with modernity remains an ongoing challenge. As Bhutan becomes more connected to the global economy and younger generations gain exposure to different lifestyles through education and technology, maintaining cultural cohesion while promoting individual freedom becomes increasingly complex.

The Buddhist philosophy at the core of GNH

Should other countries adopt the Bhutan model of having a more holistic approach to development? The fact is that the UN has passed a resolution in support of GNH and in many regions of the world the GNH index has been adopted as a measure. If countries are concerned about the holistic well-being of its people, GNH is a superior alternative to GDP. Though GDP can never be fully done away with. Western countries have a different culture and history and their motivation may be different from that of Bhutan. This has to be kept in mind before we impress upon the West to use GNH as a measure.

Buddhism is the state religion of Bhutan and about three-fourths of the population are considered to be its followers. The Buddhist notion of collective harmony, both with others and the environment, has played an important role in moulding the thinking of Bhutan. The Buddhist philosophy is clear that happiness does not come from external factors, which can only lead to unhappiness. Cultivating inner contentment is the way to happiness. It emphasizes the importance of mental and spiritual development for attaining true happiness, transcending material wealth. The cultivation of happiness is central to Buddhist philosophy and practices, and there are limitless avenues and methods prescribed in the teachings through which happiness can be achieved at the individual or collective levels. Thus, GNH focuses both on the material and spiritual well-being of the people to achieve happiness. This is the famous middle path of Buddha where extremes have to be avoided. The nine domains of GNH are extensions of Buddhist philosophy that aims to strike a balance between psychological well-being and improvement of living standards.

Since Buddhism has shaped Bhutanese thought for generations, GNH seems like the most sensible policy for this nation to employ. However, it can be pointed out that even in the ranking of countries according to the GNH index, it is countries like Finland, Norway, Sweden, Denmark and New Zealand that are ranked in the top 10 in the world. The US and many West European countries also score high on this index. This proves that GNH does bring out the crucial aspect of well-being and quality of life.

Many find it difficult to measure the degree of richness and wealth. However, from a Buddhist perspective those who are rich can be measured in terms of whether they also possess contentment or not. In the 12th century, a Chinese emperor wanted to learn who was the richest man in Tibet at that time. He was told that the yogi Milarepa was the richest. The meaning implied was that although he was materially very poor, he was extremely rich spiritually and was contented with whatever he found along the way on his spiritual journey. He was the happiest yogi of his time.

As the Buddha explained, "The best indicator of wealth is the measure of contentment found. And enlightenment is the supreme indicator for measuring happiness as well."

Achieving GNH in India: Challenges and strategies

Despite being the fourth-largest economy in the world and having one of the highest growth rates, India ranks 118th in the *WHR 2025*, improving from 126th in 2024. In terms of per capita income India is still low and is far from being a developed country.

Furthermore, India has a high degree of social and economic inequality, which lowers well-being. Along with infrastructure and industrialization, healthcare and education also require significant improvement. Low growth rates and the suffering of farmers are further problems facing the agriculture industry. Nonetheless, there are still close familial ties and a lot of community support in India.

The people of India are religious and spiritual in their outlook and tend to take a holistic view of life and historically have not attached that much importance to materialism. The younger generation's desire for higher incomes and material benefits is causing this mindset to shift. The nation's youth are no longer satisfied with the current situation. They are happy to live in a democracy with freedom of speech and fundamental rights, but they are generally dissatisfied with their material well-being when compared to the developed world, which may account for India's poor ranking in the GNH index.

India is a young nation experiencing a significant demographic dividend, but this has also resulted in low educational standards and high unemployment. Naturally the youth is dissatisfied.

In my opinion, India should employ GNH as a development indicator in addition to GDP since it is sustainable development which is currently the objective the nation must pursue.

Bhutan has been able to strike a balance between modernity and tradition on the one hand and environment and economic growth on the other. The GNH has had a significant impact in guiding the public discussion, policies and laws of Bhutan. It has provided a development framework by virtue of which Bhutan has remained reasonably equitable where the proportion of unhappy people is on the lower side given the level of per capita income. There has been quite a positive impact on the people of Bhutan because of GNH, and it is to the credit of Bhutan that happiness has been recognized as an alternative indicator to the path of development. GNH is superior to HDI and GDP for measuring happiness because it takes into account all possible factors both internal and external which account for happiness in human beings.

The only limitation appears to be that the mode of computation is very elaborate and often subjective and difficult to quantify. Indian policymakers must assess the happiness of their people according to GNH and make policies which come good on the happiness parameters.

A beginning has been made in India. In 2016, the government of Madhya Pradesh established a department of happiness called the Anand Department. It plans to run approximately 70 programmes and develop a happiness index for the state.

Responding to rising concerns about mental health, stress and emotional burnout in students, schools and universities have set up centres for happiness on their campuses. By integrating happiness as a formal subject and promoting well-being through structured programmes, these centres are fostering emotional intelligence, self-awareness and a sense of balance enabling students to thrive both academically and personally.

Since 2016, as many as 65 schools and colleges including the University of Delhi, IIT Kharagpur, IIT Delhi, IIT Roorkee, IIT Jodhpur, Delhi Technological University (DTU), several IIMs, and Amity University have already launched dedicated happiness courses and centres. These initiatives often blend scientific research, experiential learning and community engagement, creating a ripple effect that not only enhances student life but also transforms institutional culture.

On International Happiness Day in March 2025, IIT Delhi collaborated with the Rekhi Foundation for Happiness, to launch a happiness lab to address mental well-being. To cultivate happiness as a life skill, IIT Delhi offers a credit-based semester course to students in their third and fourth years.

Indian policymakers must be concerned about India's low rank in the world happiness surveys and reports. It would be beneficial for them to stop living in denial and keep challenging *WHR*'s methodology and frequently claiming a motive. Instead, they should attempt to do a thorough investigation of the potential causes of the country's low level of happiness.

4

Sustainable Development Goals 2030

A Roadmap for Happiness

We do not inherit the
Earth from our
Ancestors, we borrow it
From our children

—Native American proverb

Millennium Development Goals

The United Nations Millennium Development Goals (MDGs) are the eight goals set by the UN in September 2000 and agreed to be achieved by the year 2015. The

Millennium Declaration was signed at the September global summit held at the UN headquarters in New York where international leaders in attendance committed to combating disease, hunger, poverty, illiteracy, discrimination against women and environmental degradation. The MDGs were derived from this declaration, and specific indicators and targets were attached to them.

The UN set eight MDGs for all the nations which if achieved should lead to genuine economic development and also provide a good quality of life to all citizens. These goals were:

1. Eradicate extreme poverty and hunger
2. Achieve universal primary education
3. Promote gender equality and empower women
4. Reduce child mortality
5. Improve maternal health
6. Combat HIV/Aids, malaria and other diseases
7. Ensure environmental sustainability
8. Develop a global partnership for development

The level of achievement of these goals would be an indicator of the status of development of the nation. The global mobilization behind the MDGs has produced the most successful anti-poverty movement in history. The landmark commitment entered into by world leaders to "spare no effort to free our fellow men, women and children from the abject and dehumanizing conditions of extreme poverty" was translated into an inspiring framework of eight goals and, then, into wide-ranging practical steps that have enabled people across the world to improve their lives and their future prospects.

The global success story of the MDGs

The MDGs achieved significant success by 2015.

- The number of people living in extreme poverty fell from 1.9 billion in 1990 to 836 million in 2015. The proportion of undernourished people in developing regions dropped from 23.3 per cent to 12.9 per cent.
- The primary school enrolment rate in developing regions reached 91 per cent in 2015, up from 83 per cent in 2000.
- About two-thirds of developing countries achieved gender parity in primary education. Progress has been particularly strong in Southern Asia. Only 74 girls were enrolled in primary school for every 100 boys in 1990. By 2015, 103 girls enrolled for every 100 boys.
- The world has made enormous progress in improving child survival since 1990, reducing the under-five mortality rate by nearly half from 90 to 46 deaths per 1,000 live births in 2013.
- Between 1990 and 2015, the maternal mortality ratio was nearly halved.
- The results with MDG 5 are mixed. The target of halting and beginning to reverse the spread of HIV/AIDS has not been met although the number of new HIV infections fell by 40 per cent between 2000 and 2013.

- Between 1990 and 2015, 2.6 billion people gained access to improved drinking water, meaning the target of halving the proportion of people without access to safe water was achieved. Worldwide, 2.1 billion people gained access to improved sanitation.
- Official development assistance from wealthy countries to developing countries increased by 66 per cent in real terms between 2000 and 2014, reaching $135.2 billion.

By putting people and their immediate needs at the forefront, the MDGs reshaped decision-making in developed and developing countries alike. Yet for all the remarkable gains, inequalities persisted and that progress had been uneven. The world's poor remain overwhelmingly concentrated in some parts of the world. In 2011, nearly 60 per cent of the world's one billion extremely poor people lived in just five countries. Too many women continue to die during pregnancy or from childbirth-related complications.

Progress tends to bypass women and those who are lowest on the economic ladder or are disadvantaged because of their age, disability or ethnicity. Disparities between rural and urban areas remain pronounced.

Unswerving political will and collective, long-term effort were required to tackle the root causes and do more to integrate the economic, social and environmental dimensions of sustainable development. Accordingly, the UN General Assembly met in 2015 and brought out "a blueprint to achieve a better and more sustainable future for all people and the world by 2030". The emerging post-2015 development agenda, including the set of sustainable development goals, strived to reflect these lessons, build on the successes and put all countries, together, firmly on track towards a more prosperous, sustainable and equitable world.

Sustainable Development Goals

With 2030 as the target year, this UN resolution, also known as Agenda 2030, went into effect in 2018 following the conclusion of the MDGs in 2015. The UN came out with 17 SDGs which were divided into 169 targets and 232 indicators. The SDGs are a universal call to action established by the UN to end poverty, protect the planet and ensure prosperity for all by 2030.

Achievement of these goals is now used to measure economic and human development of nations. These SDGs are the blueprint to achieve a better and more sustainable future for all by addressing the global challenges faced by all nations.

Eradicating poverty (SDG 1)

The first goal relates to elimination of poverty of all forms. The impact of the COVID-19 pandemic, which is estimated to have caused an additional 120 million people to live in poverty globally—an alarming 23 million in India, according to a study by Azim Premjee University—has made this aim even more pertinent. This goal sought to reduce global poverty to 7 per cent in 2030. This goal has now become more difficult because of the pandemic.

Age, geographic region, sex and work status are some of the parameters used to determine the percentage of persons living below international poverty line. Each nation has to evolve its own strategy to reduce the incidence of poverty and for this they have to implement appropriate social protection systems. By 2030, the objective is to cut the percentage of people living in poverty in half and end extreme poverty, which is defined as living on less than US$3.00 a day. It also envisages ensuring that all men and women, particularly the poor and the vulnerable, have equal access to economic resources as well as basic services.

Achieving zero hunger (SDG 2)

The second goal seeks to end hunger, achieve food security, improve nutrition and promote sustainable agriculture. Agriculture productivity and the income of farmers need to be increased to achieve this goal. Resilient agriculture and food production systems will need to be evolved.

Ensuring health for all (SDG 3)

The third objective is to guarantee everyone's health and well-being. The targets are to reduce global maternal mortality to less than 70/1000 births, neonatal mortality below 12/1000 and under-5 mortality to less than 25/1000. Additionally, it pledges to stop the spread of infectious diseases, water-borne illnesses and tropical diseases like malaria and dengue. It is also necessary to guarantee universal health coverage for everyone. This target, which links health to environment, aims to significantly lower the number of illnesses and fatalities caused by dangerous substances as well as pollution and contamination of the air, water and soil by 2030.

Guaranteeing equitable quality education for all (SDG 4)

The fourth goal seeks to ensure inclusive and equitable quality education and promote lifelong learning opportunities for all. Every boy and girl must have equitable access to high-quality elementary and secondary education as well as inexpensive, high-quality technical, vocational and post-secondary education.

Adult literacy is also a focus area. Education has to be disability and gender sensitive. It is suggested that there be a significant rise in the number of competent teachers. In addition to discussing universal access to education, this goal clearly focuses on delivering high-quality education.

Empowering women (SDG 5)

Achieving equality and empowering all women is the fifth goal. It seeks to eradicate all types of discrimination and violence against women everywhere. It hopes to bring about full and efficient participation of women in the labour force and provide them with equal opportunities of leadership.

Providing universal access to safe drinking water and sanitation (SDG 6)

The sixth goal is crucial for developing nations. It aims to provide universal access to safe drinking water, sanitation and hygiene. According to the UN, 3.6 billion people, or 46 per cent of the world's population, lack properly managed sanitation, 2.3 billion people lack basic hygiene and 2.36 billion people live in water-stressed countries. The current rate of progress needs to double, as 129 countries are not on track to achieve sustainable management of water resources by 2030. A lot of emphasis has to be given on mitigating water pollution and implementing measures for recycling and reuse of water.

Delivering sustainable energy (SDG 7)

Energy is a vital sector, and the seventh goal aims to provide everyone access to affordable, reliable, sustainable and modern energy. Energy efficiency has to be improved and there has to be a much greater thrust on substituting fossil fuels with renewable energy.

Maintaining inclusive growth, innovation and reducing inequalities (SDGs 8, 9, 10)

The eighth goal focuses on economic growth and decent work, aiming to support inclusive, long-term economic growth with productive employment for all.

Goal number nine is about resilient infrastructure, promoting industry and fostering innovation. The only nation that will advance in this era of invention is the one that can foster an environment that supports it.

Goal number 10 is concerned about reduction in inequalities, which as we have seen are a major cause of unhappiness in society. It leads to social strife. Furthermore, a society's prevailing views, values and culture can lead to social inequality. Unequal political representation may be a manifestation of this. This goal also seeks to reduce disparities between nations.

Improving quality of urban development (SDG 11)

The quality of urban development is the subject of the 11th objective. It talks about developing sustainable cities and communities by making them inclusive, safe, resilient and sustainable. By 2030, the target is to provide safe and affordable housing to all and upgrade slums by providing basic services. Public transport has to be expanded and the world's cultural and natural heritage requires to be safeguarded. Municipal waste management needs to be upgraded and special attention paid to reduction of air pollution in the cities.

This goal is very clear on the importance of environment by aiming to provide universal access to safe inclusive green public spaces to all. It also aims to strengthen national and regional development planning by connecting urban, semi-urban and rural areas.

Encouraging sustainable consumption and production (SDG 12)

Goal number 12 is about implementing a 10-year framework of programme on sustainable consumption and production with developed countries taking the lead. It seeks to achieve efficient use of natural resources by reducing waste generation and increasing recycling and reusing.

Managing climate change (SDG 13) and protecting the environment (SDGs 14,15)

Goal number 13 is of great importance and the focus of all the countries is on taking urgent action to combat climate change and its impact. It seeks to incorporate climate change measures into national policies, plans and planning in order to increase resilience and adaptive ability to climate-related hazards and natural disasters in all nations. The conservation and sustainable use of seas, oceans and marine resources for sustainable development is the subject of goal number 14.

Goal number 15 seeks to protect, restore and promote sustainable use of terrestrial ecosystems, manage forests, combat desertification, and halt and reverse land degradation and loss of biodiversity.

Ensuring access to justice (SDG 16) and global partnership (SDG 17)

Goal number 16 seeks to promote peaceful and inclusive society by providing access to justice to all and building effective, accountable and inclusive development at all levels. Finally, goal number 17 is about strengthening the means of implementation and revitalizing the global partnership for sustainable development.

SDGs and happiness

The UN resolution on SDGs is extremely comprehensive and covers almost all aspects of human existence. The citizens of a nation that ranks well on the index of accomplishing these objectives will undoubtedly be happier than those who reside in nations that are falling behind. The ranking of the nations on the happiness index and their degree of SDG goal achievement support this. The UN resolution on happiness and the SDGs have similar goals and objectives.

The 2012 UN resolution adopted by the General Assembly on 28 June 2012 proclaimed 20 March as the International Day of Happiness.

Resolution adopted by the General Assembly on 28 June 2012

International Day of Happiness

The General Assembly,

Recalling its resolution 65/309 of 19 July 2011, which invites Member States to pursue the elaboration of additional measures that better capture the importance of the pursuit of happiness and well-being in development with a view to guiding their public policies,

Conscious that the pursuit of happiness is a fundamental human goal,

Recognizing the relevance of happiness and well-being as universal goals and aspirations in the lives of human beings around the world and the importance of their recognition in public policy objectives,

Recognizing also the need for a more inclusive, equitable and balanced approach to economic growth that promotes sustainable development, poverty eradication, happiness and the well-being of all peoples,

1. *Decides* to proclaim 20 March the International Day of Happiness;
2. *Invites* all Member States, organizations of the UN system and other international and regional organizations, as well as civil society, including NGOs and individuals, to observe the International Day of Happiness in an appropriate manner, including through education and public awareness-raising activities;
3. *Requests* the Secretary-General to bring the present resolution to the attention of all Member States, organizations of the United Nations system and civil society organizations for appropriate observance.

118th plenary meeting

28 June 2012

How countries have fared with Agenda 2030

The SDGs aim to create a pattern of economic development which ensures inclusive and sustainable growth. The goal of public policy is best served by making people happy and this is possible only if all sections of society are included in the process of growth and also the interests of the future generations are taken into consideration. The SDGs have been designed after due deliberation to bring about holistic development.

Global performance

- European countries continue to lead in the SDG index—19 of the top 20 countries are from Europe.
- Finland, Sweden and Denmark are the top three countries on the SDG index.
- East and South Asia have outperformed all other global regions in terms of SDG progress, demonstrating the fastest progress since 2015 largely due to socio-economic development.

Among India's neighbours, Bhutan ranks 74th (70.5), Nepal 85th (68.6), Bangladesh 114th (63.9) and Pakistan 140th (57). Maritime neighbours Maldives and Sri Lanka stand at 53rd and 93rd places respectively.

China is ranked 49th with a score of 74.4. And the US stands at 44th with 75.2 points.

India's performance

India's SDG performance is currently at 67, ranking 99th out of 167 nations in the *2025 Sustainable Development Report*. This marks a significant improvement from its previous ranking of 112th in 2023. India has been ranked among the top 100 countries in the index for the first time since this data began to be published from 2016.

NITI Aayog is the nodal institution for achieving SDGs in the country, leading the 2030 Agenda with the spirit of cooperative and competitive federalism. NITI Aayog has created an SDG index to measure the performance of the various Indian states. It is encouraging to see that the Indian government has made achieving the SDGs a high priority since they are the most likely to increase national happiness. It monitors the performance of states/UTs through the SDG India index, north-eastern region district SDG index, and multidimensional poverty index. It promotes SDG localization and encourages a competitive spirit among states and UTs. The SDG India Index 2023–24 report by NITI Aayog provides a comprehensive overview of India's progress towards achieving the SDGs. While some states and UTs have made significant strides in specific SDG areas, others continue to address critical developmental gaps. By highlighting these disparities, the index supports targeted interventions and fosters both competition and collaboration to expedite SDG achievement nationwide.

NITI Aayog has concluded that India has done well in eradicating both absolute and multidimensional poverty, with about 410 million people emerging from poverty over the past 20 years. The trend indicates that the SDG objective of eradicating poverty will be accomplished by 2030. As regards the second SDG goal of achieving zero hunger, it is debatable whether people in India are going hungry without food but the country has a very high rate of malnutrition and undernourishment, as evidenced by the statistics on stunting and wasting and it seems unlikely that this SDG goal will be met by 2030.

This would adversely impact the productivity of Indian youth and overall economic development of the country. The policymakers of India must focus on removing malnutrition if they want to create a happy society. It is not encouraging to note that India ranks 104th on the global hunger index scale.

Happiness is directly correlated with the third SDG of good health and well-being, and despite some ground-breaking programmes like the Ayushman Bharat insurance policy, India's performance in this area is far from ideal. The out-of-pocket expenditure in India is still about 40 per cent, making this a major cause for poverty. Further, the rural primary health and wellness centres are still suffering from shortage of doctors and equipment.

Specifically, there has been insufficient progress in eradicating non-communicable diseases including diabetes and cancer. The status of universal health coverage is mediocre. Public policy in India has to prioritize healthcare in the coming years. The expenditure on public health in India is currently about 1.9 per cent of GDP, which is below the target of 2.5 per cent as per the National Health Policy 2017. Despite this, the government has increased its health expenditure to 1.84 per cent of GDP for FY26, reflecting a commitment to improving healthcare infrastructure and services. It is approximately 17 per cent in US and 5 per cent in China.

Similarly, though the literacy rate in India has improved as also the enrolment rate but at the primary level there is still a problem of dropouts and lower level of enrolment and attendance among girl students. The quality of education is not of the desired level. Indian public policy must prioritize the provision of high-quality education. The new education policy is a welcome step in this direction but the focus has to be on proper and time-bound execution.

Likewise, the fifth goal of gender equality is likewise unlikely to be achieved in a timely manner, especially as women's labour force participation rate is significantly lower than men's, despite an increase in the number of female pupils.

In terms of political empowerment, the participation of women in municipal bodies is enough, but not in parliament, where a law was recently passed to give women a 33 per cent reservation. However, it will take some time for this law to take effect. India is also falling behind in developing sustainable cities and meeting all of its fundamental necessities.

State-wise performance on SDGs

Many state governments have begun keeping an eye on the progress of SDGs after realizing how important they are. According to data from the Government of India's

Ministry of Statistics, Kerala leads all Indian states in reaching the SDGs with a score of 75 compared to the country's average of 66. With a score of 74, Tamil Nadu and Himachal Pradesh are ranked second. States like Uttar Pradesh and Bihar need to perform better, whereas Goa, Andhra Pradesh, Karnataka and Uttarakhand are rated fourth.

Goal-wise, Tamil Nadu is in the forefront of SDG of healthcare, while Kerala is at the forefront of SDG of quality education. Odisha has made significant strides in empowering women and Himachal Pradesh is a model for environmental sustainability (SDG 13). Punjab is the granary of India and shows the way regarding food security (SDG 2) while Rajasthan has done commendable work in giving access to clean water and sanitation (SDG 6). West Bengal has done well in reducing in inequalities (SDG 10). The laggard states have to improve to ensure that the entire country moves forward to achieve the SDG goals by 2030 and create a just, equitable and happy society.

How far a country has come in achieving the overall objective of these goals can be measured by using the metric of subjective well- being.

Subjective well-being: The science of happiness

Subjective well-being is a widely used metric that measures how individuals experience and evaluate their lives. This considers a number of variables that affect joy and happiness as well as those that lead to tension and anxiety. Subjective well-being is the scientific term for happiness and life satisfaction—thinking and feeling that your life is going well, not badly. As the name implies, SWB is a subjective measure that rates happiness on a relative scale. Economic well-being is determined by comparing the perceived well-being of various nations or communities.

People's levels of SWB are influenced by both internal factors, such as personality and outlook, and external factors, such as the society in which they live. Some of the major determinants of SWB are a person's inborn temperament, the quality of their social relationships, the societies they live in and their ability to meet their basic needs. In other words, people high in SWB seem to be healthier and function more effectively compared to people who are chronically stressed, depressed or angry. Thus, happiness does not just feel good, but it is good for people and for those around them. When people describe what they most want out of life, happiness is almost always on the list, and very frequently it is at the top of the list. When people describe what they want in life for their children, they frequently mention health and wealth, occasionally they mention fame or success—but they almost always mention happiness. People will claim that whether their kids are wealthy and work in some prestigious occupation or not, "I just want my kids to be happy."

Happiness appears to be one of the most important goals for people, if not the most important. But what is it, and how do people get it?

Edward Diener in his paper "Happiness: The Science of Subjective Well-Being" describes happiness or SWB as a process—it results from certain internal and external causes, and in turn it influences the way people behave, as well as their physiological states. Thus, high SWB is not just a pleasant outcome but is an important factor in our future success.

Philosophers have debated the nature of happiness for thousands of years, but scientists have recently discovered that happiness means different things. The three major types of happiness are high life satisfaction, frequent positive feelings and infrequent negative feelings. "Subjective well-being" is the label given by scientists to the various forms of happiness taken together.

A person who is extremely content with his life or career because it provides him with a strong sense of self-worth or a solid salary is an example of life contentment. In a similar vein, enjoying life and feeling affection for others is an example of having pleasant emotions. Supportive friends, engaging work and her extroverted personality could all contribute to this.

A person who is rarely sad or angry and has few chronic worries, either due to a positive outlook or because his life goals are in harmony can be described as happy. From these one can deduce that happiness is a combination of various factors. Some people may have one type of happiness but not another. For example, a person may have a very high level of income but his health may be bad. In fact, in life rarely would you get a person who is fully happy on all fronts. In everybody's life there is something missing. There are happy and sad times in every life. However, SWB takes into account all these factors to consider whether a person is more happy than sad.

Some people experience all three elements of happiness—they are very satisfied, enjoy life and have only a few worries or other unpleasant emotions. While some unfortunate people are missing all three. There are others who show a different pattern, for example, who really enjoy life but also experience a lot of stress, anger, and worry. And there are those who have fun, but who are dissatisfied and believe they are wasting their lives. Because there are several components to happiness, each with somewhat different causes, there is no magic single cure-all that creates all forms of SWB. This means that to be happy, individuals must acquire each of the different elements that cause it.

What are the factors that influence subjective well-being?

These could be external as well as internal. A person may be poor and living with ill health but could still be happy depending upon his general outlook towards life. However, if a person is healthy and financially well off he is likely to be happier. One could argue that people's inclinations toward happiness differ.

The internal causes for SWB have been defined by experts as top-down influences. Among the internal factors that contribute to happiness are innate temperament, personality, outlook and resilience. There are those who always focus on the brighter side of life while others keep bemoaning their misfortunes.

The external factors, which are sometimes referred to as "bottom-up influences", can be explained by an individual living in a desirable community and possessing adequate financial and social resources.

What makes us happy?

A person's level of happiness is influenced by the society in which they live. When evaluating his level of happiness, a person considers not only his relationships, achievements, setbacks and other personal aspects, but also the happiness of the people in his community.

Some societies are happier than others. Happiness index shows that people living in North America and Europe have a higher level of satisfaction than those living in Africa. Conflicts or situation of war or violence in society always lead to lower level of SWB.

Relationships very often are more important than money in determining the level of SWB of a person or society. Money is undoubtedly crucial as having too little of it can make one unhappy, but having too much of it has diminishing returns. For example, Diener and Seligman have found that the US has not experienced an increase in life satisfaction over the past decades even though income levels have doubled. In actuality, pursuing money excessively often results in dissatisfaction. You only need to glance around to discover that a lot of billionaires are dissatisfied because they constantly compare their income to that of individuals who are wealthier than them.

Similarly, it is not unusual to find a person with limited income being high on the happiness scale. The reasons for his happiness could be his family, friends, religion, his work and his general positive temperament. However, it is also true that if the income level of such a person increases, he will be able to afford better things in life thereby improving his level of life satisfaction.

Psychological influences like aspirations, social comparisons and adaptation also have a bearing on a person's level of happiness. An excessively lofty goal may inspire someone for a while, but if it is not fulfilled, it leads to discontent. The goal is to have challenging aspirations but also to be able to adapt to what actually happens in life.

Do problems cause unhappiness? If that were true, there would be no happy person on this planet as everybody has his share of problems and failures. How people view their lives, overcome setbacks and adjust to disappointments have a bearing on their happiness quotient.

People's degree of happiness is mostly determined by how they initially respond to positive or negative circumstances and how they change over time. A person may first be shocked by a negative life experience, but how well he adjusts to it over time determines how happy he is.

Thus, happiness comes not to people who never have problems—there are no such individuals—but to people who are able to bounce back from failures and adapt to disappointments.

Why being happy matters

Happy people are optimistic and live a healthier and longer life. They have supportive social relationships and are willing to give as much to their relationships as they take from it. Any organization with contented management and staff will see increased production since happy people are more productive. Additionally, contented individuals donate to charities and assist others at work.

Subjective well-being can be gauged through surveys or self-reports. Individuals may be asked to identify their SWB by responding to numerical scales. On a scale of 1 to 7, where 1 represents severe disagreement and 7 represents strong agreement, a person can be asked if he feels that his life is meaningful and purposeful. This allows for the computation of the SWB level and gives rise to several questions. Is it feasible for someone to advance on the SWB scale? It is undoubtedly the case, yet each individual may have a different contributing aspect.

Does SWB or GDP measure up?

We may conclude that SWB is superior to GDP as a measure of happiness as it focuses on multiple dimensions of the lives of people. The above discussion shows that SWB measure is based on surveys and considers both external and internal factors. It takes into account various factors influencing happiness and causing stress and worry. It ranks the SWB of people on a relative scale and is based on the perception of people. It has been found that people with high SWB are healthier and more productive.

A high level of SWB creates a positive feeling which can be equated with a high level of life satisfaction or happiness. Relationships are a critical factor contributing to SWB. Conflicts and wars lead to lower level of SWB among people living in nations impacted by them. When it comes to gauging people's quality of life, SWB is unquestionably better than GDP.

OECD Better life index

The OECD has also computed its own index called the better life index (BLI) to assess the life satisfaction of people in various countries. This index says that there is more to life than the cold numbers of GDP and economic statistics. It evaluates nations based on 11 criteria that the OECD has determined are crucial for improving material living standards and quality of life.

In comparison to 2010, when every OECD nation was experiencing a financial crisis, it concludes that life satisfaction has increased in 2020.

People are living longer and safe lives with life expectancy having crossed 80 years. Incomes and jobs are on the rise with the employment rate increasing. Both average homicide rate and the number of traffic fatalities have decreased.

However, the OECD also shows that there are differences between population groups within countries and also between member countries. There is still a lot of room for improvement. Approximately 40 per cent of households are financially insecure and fear slipping into poverty if their regular monthly income is not received for three months, whereas 12 per cent of people in OECD countries live in relative poverty. Twenty per cent of households spend more than 40 per cent of their disposable income on housing. Relationships are becoming less important to people, and the amount of time spent with friends and family is decreasing alarmingly.

Older people are likely to lack social support as compared to younger people. Many people suffer from low emotional well-being and despair. The number of deaths due to suicide, alcohol abuse and drug overdose has gone up. Inequalities have gone up. According to the OECD report, bold and deliberate investments in the resources that support long-term welfare are necessary to guarantee the continued prosperity of people and the world.

The OECD report also says that only one in three people feel that they have a say in what the government does and less than half of citizens across OECD countries trust their institutions. Women hold just one-third of all seats in OECD parliaments, and hence inclusive decision making remains a distant goal.

The OECD index is called "How's life" and it measures well-being across 38 OECD countries and four partner countries. It has a set of over 80 indicators. It measures well-being across 15 dimensions which are income and wealth, housing, work and job quality, health, knowledge and skills, environmental quality,

SWB, safety, work-life balance, social connections, civic engagement, economic capital, natural capital, human capital and social capital.

The OECD's 38-member countries span the world, from North America and South America to Europe and Asia-Pacific. It includes countries like Australia, Austria, Belgium, Canada, Chile, Colombia, Denmark and Czech Republic. It is clear that the OECD index is a much more comprehensive measure of well-being than GDP. Economic growth is clearly essential for social development but measuring it exclusively by economic factors ignores important social and environment factors that influence people's quality of life.

Aside from GDP per capita, sustainable development, financial transparency and the percentage of spending on human or military capital are economic indicators that provide a deeper understanding of the state of the populace. Well-being is also influenced by environmental variables such as pollution levels, biodiversity protection, climate change reaction, and energy and water availability.

Conclusion

Thus, we see that all over the world people are realizing that GDP does not give a fair measure of well-being and various indices are being developed. The point to note is that the focus has to be on the human being rather than just pure statistics.

We have seen that when evaluating a nation's level of happiness, a number of quality of life metrics outperform GDP. However, GDP cannot be eliminated. It is a crucial indicator of economic expansion. The only caution is to take into account other happiness metrics in addition to GDP in order to obtain a more accurate view of people's quality of life.

5

A Deep Dive into World Happiness Reports (2012–2025)

Mapping the Evolution of Happiness as an Important Measure for Economic Development

"This year's report [2025] pushes us to look beyond traditional determinants like health and wealth. It turns out that sharing meals and trusting others are even stronger predictors of wellbeing than expected."— Jan-Emmanuel De Neve, director of Oxford's Wellbeing Research Centre and an editor of the World Happiness Report

How happy are people today? Were people happier in the past? How satisfied with their lives are people in different societies? And how do our living conditions affect all of this?

These are difficult questions to answer, but they are questions that undoubtedly matter for each of us personally. Indeed, today, life satisfaction and happiness are central research areas in the social sciences, including mainstream economics.

Social scientists often recommend that measures of SWB should augment the usual measures of economic prosperity, such as GDP per capita. But how can happiness be measured? Are there reliable comparisons of happiness across time and space that can give us clues regarding what makes people declare themselves "happy"?

The *WHR* employs a comprehensive methodology that combines survey data, statistical analysis and various indicators to assess happiness levels across countries. It is the world's foremost publication on global well-being and how to improve it. The *WHR* is a well-known source of cross-country data and research on self-reported life satisfaction.

The underlying source of the happiness scores in the *WHR* is the Gallup World Poll (GWP)—a set of nationally representative surveys undertaken in more than 160 countries in over 140 languages. The main life evaluation question asked in the poll is: "Please imagine a ladder, with steps numbered from 0 at the bottom to 10 at the top. The top of the ladder represents the best possible life for you and the bottom of the ladder represents the worst possible life for you. On which step of the ladder would you say you personally feel you stand at this time?" (This is known as the Cantril Ladder.) The report measures SWB using the Cantril Ladder to reflect people's own views, rather than external judgements. The goal is to free respondents to evaluate their own well-being. Subjective well-being is a concept of well-being that focus on evaluations from the perspective of the people whose lives are being evaluated rather than from some objective viewpoint.

The map plots the average answer that survey respondents provided to this question in different countries. As with the steps of the ladder, values in the map range from 0 to 10. The *WHR* has increased global interest in measuring happiness. The report is part of a movement to look into factors such as well-being to attend to the needs of countries when it comes to policy-making.

The *WHR* is a partnership of Gallup, the Wellbeing Research Centre at the University of Oxford, the UN Sustainable Development Solutions Network and the *WHR*'s editorial board. The Wellbeing Research Centre is an interdisciplinary research group focussed on the empirical study of well-being. From 2024, it is the publisher of the annual world happiness report.

World Happiness Report 2012

The first *WHR* was published on 1 April 2012 and written by John Heliwell, Richard Layard and Jeffrey Sachs. It stated that we were living in an age of stark contradictions where technological breakthroughs have enhanced economic productivity and also made quality of life of people much better. Yet a lot of this had been achieved by destruction of the natural environment. Though people enjoyed a better life, they were not immune to the ills of modern lifestyle diseases. It had to be evaluated whether material advancement that had taken place led to greater happiness of people by promoting social justice and reducing their suffering. We were in the Anthropocene age where humans are shaping their own destinies. It urged us to focus on sustainable development which means a combination of human well-being, social inclusion and environmental sustainability.

The report discussed the Easterlin Paradox in detail and questioned the dominant profit motive in the capitalist system, raising questions on whether we need to give more importance to cooperation, trust and community. For instance, the studies claimed that Finland's exceptional educational system was a result of its schools' promotion of equality and a sense of community. This analysis makes it quite evident that we need to reconsider the financial foundations of happiness and well-being.

It observed that though the concept of happiness is a subjective one, it can be objectively measured and assessed. The *WHR*s are a step in this direction to carry out a scientific study of happiness. It analysed two broad measurements of happiness—affective happiness and evaluative happiness. Affective happiness is the realm of emotions and immediate responses to events, such as joy or sadness. It is often associated with activities like laughter, fun and parties.

In contrast, evaluative happiness is a more systemic matter, reflecting a person's overall appraisal of life and satisfaction with their life. It is often linked to good health, sufficient income, social cohesion and safety. The distinction between these two types of happiness is crucial for understanding the multifaceted nature of human well-being and the factors that contribute to it. The report observed that happiness can be achieved through better designing and delivery of public services.

By introducing the concept of GNH, Bhutan took the lead in declaring happiness as the goal of human life and public policy. The SDGs also intend to bring about comprehensive development by ending extreme poverty, bringing about environmental sustainability, ensuring social income and good governance. It is believed that the data so collected by the *WHR*s will improve micro economic policymaking and service delivery. It recognized how both external and personal factors determine well-being.

The report goes on to state that in poorer countries absolute income was important whereas in richer countries it was the relative income that was important. Factors like social trust, quality of work, freedom of choice and political participation also influenced the degree of happiness.

It identified education as a significant factor in contributing to happiness. The higher the level of education in a society the more likely it is to be a happier one as people have more opportunities and higher incomes.

The *WHR 12* stated that happy societies would be those who work towards reduction of economic, social and political inequalities.

As we have seen, happiness is a complex phenomenon which depends on a huge range of influences, a large number of which can be influenced by government policy.

The report discussed how happiness could be compared across individuals, nations and cultures. There were likely to be differences in the responses of people in a survey of SWB depending upon cultural differences. However, they analysed the data drawn from different nations and cultures and found that it appeared to be influenced by the same factors and to the same extent. The gross national commonality[1] of the correlates of life evaluation was found to be significant.

Changing aspirations, adaptation and relativities created a problem in using happiness data as a measure of quality of life over time. Still, it was possible to analyse the happiness level across communities and over time. Some scholars argued that human capacities for adaptation are so strong that even major changes in life circumstances do not have a lasting impact on subjective well-being.

The necessity of being concerned with happiness arose from the fact that it was possible to take measures to improve the level of happiness of individuals as well as a nation. Research revealed that happiness was a useful predictor of the public policy actions required to raise happiness levels. It is in this context that the GNH framework developed by Bhutan assumed great significance. An analysis of the SWB data was required to find out what factors were leading to its low levels. There had always been a constraint of public expenditure on public policy measures that could be taken. However, it would be worthwhile to

---

1. This is an expression used by *GHR* to show that despite different nations having different cultures their responses to the happiness surveys were influenced by identical factors.

analyse the happiness per unit of public expenditure on various aspects of public policy.

Costa Rica, Denmark, Ireland, Norway and Finland were ranked as the top five countries in terms of life satisfaction. India's rank was 118th out of 157 countries. This happiness index is based on the survey results on scale of 0 to 10 and originates from the Bhutan GNH index. The main parameters in this index were GDP per capita, social support, healthy life expectancy, freedom to make life choices, generosity and perception of corruption.

The report concluded that happiness could be measured as a public policy tool and that SWB had an important bearing on policy debates.

World Happiness Report 2013

The *WHR 2013* begins by talking about objectives of public policy especially in the light of the sustainable development goals. In 2011, the UN passed a resolution inviting member countries to measure the happiness of their people and to use this to help them guide their public policy. Since happiness had been the aspiration for every human being, it was also a measure of social progress. The report concluded by making a significant statement that there was a worldwide demand that public policy be more closely aligned with what really matters with people in their lives.

It was found that despite the negative effect of the 2008 financial crisis, the world except Europe appeared happier and more generous over the last five years. The South Asian data showed a significant drop in average life evaluation.

Box 5.1: Risk Factors and Protective Factors for Mental Health

Level of determinant	*Risk factors*		*Protective factors*
	Low self-esteem	↔	Self-esteem, confidence
Individual attributes	Emotional immaturity	↔	Ability to manage stress and adversity
	Difficulties in communicating	↔	Communication skills
	Medical illness, substance abuse	↔	Physical health, fitness
	Loneliness, bereavement	↔	Social support of family and friends
	Neglect, family conflict	↔	Good parenting/family interaction
Social circumstances	Exposure to violence/abuse	↔	Physical security and safety
	Low income and poverty	↔	Economic security
	Difficulties or failure at school	↔	Scholastic achievement
	Work stress, unemployment	↔	Satisfaction and success at work
	Poor access to basic services	↔	Equality of access to basic services
Environmental factors	Injustice and discrimination	↔	Social justice, tolerance, integration
	Exposure to war or disaster	↔	Physical security and safety

Source: World Health Report 2013

Though higher economic growth and greater generosity had a positive impact it was offset by factors like declining social support, less perceived freedom to make life choices and inequality in the distribution of happiness.

Denmark, Norway, Switzerland, Netherlands and Sweden were the top five happy countries. India was ranked at 111 with a score of 4.772 out of a total of 156 countries.

The *WHR 2013* indicated the factors that could influence the level of happiness and growth of countries.

The report identified mental illness especially depression as the single biggest cause of misery. Mental illness affected about 10 per cent of the world population at any one time. Worldwide, depression and anxiety accounted for up to a fifth of all disabilities. Since mental illness has a cost to it in terms of loss of output and employment and increase in expenditure on healthcare, the report attempted to understand how it can be prevented as seen in Box 5.1.

The conclusion was that countries need to spend a higher proportion of their health budget on mental health.

The report stated that happiness influenced SWB and the reverse was also true. Subjective well-being has a clear relationship with future health, mortality, productivity and income. Happiness leads to positive feelings and greater cooperation, motivation and creativity which are instrumental to success in professional as well as personal life. It suggested balancing the economic measures of growth with measures of SWB to ensure that economic progress leads to improvement across various life domains. It recommended well-being be placed at the heart of the policy if people were to be happier.

This *WHR* advocated restoring virtue ethics in the quest for happiness. Happiness typically is defined in a different manner by economists who link it to higher income and consumption; sociologist focus on the quality of social support while psychologists talk about the importance of personality traits and state of mind. There is, however, the ethical dimension of happiness which had been overlooked. Philosophers have suggested that virtue ethics is an important determinant of happiness. Virtue ethics is a philosophical approach that emphasizes the development of good character traits as a determinant of happiness.

The growth of the modern economy led to an excessive emphasis on economic growth which resulted in an overall improvement in the material life of people. However, non-economic factors got ignored in the process. There was evidence to show that aggressive pursuit of higher income in the US came at a cost of declining social capital, mental well-being and ethical behaviour. Happiness had to be defined in a broader context with the role of virtue ethics also taken into account.

The report discussed how virtue and happiness were interlinked in ancient traditions. Moderation and compassion were accepted as better paths to happiness than merely indulgence in sensual pleasures and acquiring material possessions. Buddha clearly saw a clear connection between desire and human suffering. He provided the ethical framework for living life. Like him, other religious leaders have emphasized living in peace with yourself and harmony with all other aspects of creation around you for a happy life.

The *WHR* stated how Aristotle too talked of virtue and ethics as being essential for happiness. He too was an advocate of the middle path. He said that following a path of virtue, which he called Eudemonia, promoted happiness and attended to not only the individual's well-being but also the community's harmony. The Christian doctrine of happiness views it in the context of servicing of God's will and advocates living properly on earth in line with the will of God. The Christian church identified four cardinal virtues of prudence, justice, fortitude and temperance and three theological virtues of faith, hope and charity.

As consumerism increased in society, virtue ethics got replaced with the utility doctrine of economists who became new "worldly philosophers". In the age of unrestrained consumerism, utility function measures happiness from buying a basket of goods. The *WHR* identified this as materialistic thinking which focused on the relationship of individuals with commodities. It assumed that market commodities gave pain or pleasure to consumers. In the mid-19th century, this was the main focus of the economists and they related happiness with this.

Thereafter, happiness began to acquire a material connotation and was increasingly getting associated with acquiring more and more personal wealth. This ethos continued for around one century but counter currents began to evolve which put forward the values of social justice, redistribution, ecological sustainability, social capital and psychological detachment from consumerism. It was increasingly felt that hyper-commercialism impacted social capital which is a key factor in well-being. Soon modern societies began to realize that an excessive desire for wealth and consumption leads to personal unhappiness, addictions, ill health and other psychological, social and physical problems.

It was soon recognized that happiness was not merely an economic phenomenon but was affected by social and psychological factors. The question remained: to what extent ethics related to happiness. And how virtue ethics could guide public policy.

Another chapter argued using well-being as a guide to policy. Countries were using data on well-being to improve their policymaking even though there were lot of political and practical difficulties in this. However, the conclusion was that this approach led to a better public policy. This implied that one will have to move away from GDP being the sole determinant of growth and well-being. Different governments were using various indicators and assigning different weightage to measure SWB and design policy according to that. Policy interventions had to consider raising both well-being and incomes. In most cases there need not be a trade-off between the two. Future generations would be much better off if sustainable development policies are formulated but often politicians are more concerned with the present as they have to gather votes. Bhutan had taken the lead by adopting the objective of maximizing gross national happiness.

The report had observed that these were early days of using well-being to drive policy decisions, and techniques to do so were still being refined. Consensus among international institutions in ways of measuring well-being was identified to be a critical factor. The focus should be on understanding which policy would raise well-being in a sustainable way. The evolution from the GDP era to the well-being era has started.

The OECD developed its own guidelines on measuring subjective well-being. These guidelines were published on 20 March 2013 and constitute the first international handbook on the measurement of subjective well-being. Its approach to measuring SWB covered a wide range of subjects rather than only happiness. The approach encompassed the following three elements:

1. *Life evaluation:* This is a continuous assessment of one's existence, reflecting on how well one's life aligns with personal values and purpose. It involves reflecting on past experiences, relationships and decisions to gain insights and derive meaning from life.
2. *Affect*: It is measured through emotional reactions and feelings, often assessed against a specific point in time.
3. *Eudemonia*: It refers to a sense of purpose and meaning in life, which can be influenced by personal values and life circumstances.

The report stated that these concepts together help individuals understand their well-being and the quality of their lives.

Box 5.2: OECD Core Measures of Subjective Well-Being

PRIMARY MEASURE

The following question asks how satisfied you feel, on a scale from 0 to 10. Zero means you feel 'not at all satisfied' and 10 means you feel 'completely satisfied'.

A1. Overall, how satisfied are you with life as a whole these days? *[0–10]*

ADDITIONAL CORE MEASURES

The following question asks how worthwhile you feel the things you do in your life are, on a scale from 0 to 10. Zero means you feel the things you do in your life are 'not at all worthwhile', and 10 means 'completely worthwhile'.

A2. Overall, to what extent do you feel the things you do in your life are worthwhile? *[0–10]*

The following questions ask about how you felt yesterday on a scale from 0 to 10. Zero means you did not experience the feeling 'at all' yesterday while 10 means you experienced the feeling 'all of the time' yesterday. I will now read out a list of ways you might have felt yesterday.

A3. How about happy? *[0–10]*

A4. How about worried? *[0–10]*

A5. How about depressed? *[0–10]*

Source: OECD, 2013

The OECD approach took into account two elements which have to be measured. The first was the primary measure of life evaluation which was the absolute minimum required to measure subjective well-being. The second element consisted of a short series of affect questions and experimental eudemonic questions. An example is cited in Box 5.2.

Measuring SWB in a consistent manner required not just using a common set of questions but also taking into account a range of issues in survey design and implementation. The

SWB measure will almost always need to be collected through sample surveys.

The OECD guidelines played a critical role in the measurement of SWB but were not the final word on the subject. Different countries are using different statistics and surveys to measure subjective well-being. The report mentioned that these measures will evolve further to get better results of subjective well-being.

The last chapter of the *WHR 2013* tested the links between the human development and life satisfaction. It stated that it had been established that data on SWB and in particular on life evaluation could help answer important questions about human development. The definition of human development was flexible and open-ended, but the HDI developed by the *HDR* in 1990 came up with a series of indicators to understand human development which included education, health and command over resources and participation, human security, equity and sustainability.

The authors of the report observed that the HDI developed by Amartya Sen and Mahbub Ul Haq was considered the best measure and it challenged the hegemony of GDP in development discourse. It has shown that many countries may experience good economic growth in terms of GDP, but their performance in the social parameters of health and education may not be so good. The report established a link between human development and happiness as many of the determinants of happiness were also central to human development. Countries with higher HDI were those with more effective government.

The *WHR* demonstrated that most of the key factors that together explain happiness levels across the world were also classical human development variables. In other words, factors generally used to explain human development are equally applicable to explaining happiness.

This *WHR* focused on the fundamental drivers of happiness and highlighted how these factors explain world rankings.

The *World Happiness Report 2014* was not published.

World Happiness Report 2015

In the very first chapter of the report, it was mentioned how happiness was increasingly becoming accepted as an appropriate measure of social progress and as a goal of public policy. Many European countries had started collecting SWB data and national leaders are using this as a guide for important policy decisions. In 2014, the UK launched What Works Centre for Wellbeing dedicated to making policies and services to bring about well-being. (The centre closed in 2024 due to lack of government funding.)

The UAE made happiness and well-being the central objective of its national agenda. The Dubai Plan 2021, which was launched in 2014, stated that the first objective of the plan was achieving happiness of people. Many sub-national governments are also measuring subjective well-being. The UN had adopted the SDGs in 2015 and it became clear that all countries would make sustainable development a priority.

Happiness and well-being are terms that are often used interchangeably but there is a difference between them. Happiness is the experience a person feels of pleasure, joy or positivity. This is often linked to the mood of a person. Well-being is a broader and deeper concept that refers to how well a person's life is going on as a whole. It is multifaceted, encompassing relationships, social support, meaning and purpose of life, and physical and mental health. It is not only about feeling well; it is about living well.

This report tried to understand how well-being differed by gender, region and age. It also accounted for differences in life evaluation among countries on the basis of per capita GDP, healthy years of life expectancy, social support, trust, perceived freedom to make life decision and generosity.

The *WHR 2015* stated that if the aim of policy was to increase happiness, policymakers would have to evaluate their policy options in a different manner. Any new policy should now be measured in terms of the impact it has on the change in the happiness level of the population. Any increase in public expenditure would have to be viewed in the light of the happiness that it could generate. This would be a new form of cost-benefit analysis as money alone would not be the measure of benefit. The report used an approach based on "quality adjusted life years" as the ultimate measure of benefit. This approach was in its infancy.

There was also a chapter on neuroscience of happiness which highlighted four supports for well-being:

1. sustaining positive emotion
2. recovering from negative emotion
3. empathy and altruism
4. pro-social behaviour and mind wandering

The report drew two lessons from this. The first was the identification of the four elements which were not commonly researched and the second was that these emotions were capable of being transformed through training and experience. Accordingly, training programmes were being developed to cultivate mindfulness, kindness and generosity. In essence, happiness and well-being were skills which could be enhanced by training.

There was a specific chapter on happiness of children as they comprised one-third of the global population. It explored the aspects of child development that were most important in determining whether the child will grow up as a happy person. It came to the conclusion that emotional development of children was the best predictor of future happiness and academic achievement the worst. Millions of children all over the world were suffering from mental health issues, which become a key determinant of their satisfaction level as adults. The report suggested key steps needed to attend to mental health problems among children as prevention was important than cure. The school had a major role to play in this and it requires the involvement of parents and children. The *WHR* suggested that children should be taught life skills using evidence-based materials to empower them effectively. Evidence-based life skills education focuses on developing self-regulation and decision-making and social skills, which are crucial for their overall well-being and future success. It emphasized that both schools and healthcare systems should give priority to the well-being of children.

Another chapter attempted to keep alive within modernity the tradition of a civil life based on friendship and a more socialized idea of person and community. It brought out the importance of social relations in experiencing happiness. The chapter recommended changes to democratic mechanisms to allow human capacity to have more space for pro-social action. It stated that happiness required real participation of citizens and not merely voting at the polling booth. The report said that to be pro-social implied that individuals make decisions for the common good that may be in conflict with short-run egoistic incentives.

Pro-social behaviour, which includes honesty, benevolence, cooperation and trustworthiness, is the key to achieving the best outcome for society. Societies with a high level of social capital are conducive to pro-social behaviour. High social capital raises well-being by promoting social support systems, generosity and voluntarism, and honesty in public administration. The report discussed various pathways to higher social capital including education, professional course of conduct and public policy that aim to narrow income inequalities.

Switzerland followed by Iceland, Denmark, Norway, Canada and Finland emerged as the top five countries in the world happiness ranking. The five countries at the bottom were Rwanda, Benin, Syria, Burundi and Tog. India was ranked at 117, which should have been an eye-opener for its policymakers.

This report emphasized that happiness should dictate public policy.

World Happiness Report 2016

The report focused on the inequality of well-being, which is different from economic inequality. The report observed that people were happier living in societies where there was less inequality of happiness. For the first time, a *WHR* gave a special role to the measurement and consequences of inequality in the distribution of well-being among countries and regions. It argued that the inequality of well-being provided a broader measure of inequality.

This report talked about ushering in more equal societies. Sustainable development should be the aim of all countries. SDGs bring about a balanced approach of growth which would ensure well-being of present and future generations and lead to a higher level of happiness in society.

In another chapter of the report it was argued that the world needed an ethical system which was both convincing and inspiring. A global decline in the impact of religious ethics does not mean that we should become less ethical. The report puts forward the principle of greatest happiness that can provide the ethical basis of society by bringing about happiness of self and others. Merely having a principle was not enough and secular organizations were required to work as forums where people could meet regularly for upliftment and mutual support. Even the Dalai Lama has said that religion is no longer an adequate basis for ethics and secular ethics are required to supplement it.

The UN adopted the SDGs in 2015 which provide a roadmap for development to be pursued by all nations by 2030. The SDGs offer a comprehensive approach to well-being incorporating economic, social and environmental objectives. They aim to help countries to achieve a more balanced approach to development. The authors of the report stated that in the recent past they have seen countries trying to maximize economic growth by ignoring its impact on the environment and the society. The recent climate change negotiations at the international level are the consequence of this phenomenon.

The question that arose was what exactly constituted happiness. The report discussed various theories of happiness and talked about the following six dimensions of happiness:

1. *Mindfulness*—this emphasizes character rather than objective circumstances. Attitudes, values, habits and virtues are important for happiness.
2. *Consumerism*—the individual is seen as a rational consumer who wants to maximize his individual utility.
3. *Economic freedom*—this is about personal freedom of choice.
4. *Dignity of work*—the quality of life at work and the scope for innovation and creation.

5. *Good governance*—a system with ensures justice for all.
6. *Social trust*—living harmoniously with each other.

The SDG 2030 takes into consideration the aforementioned characteristics.

In another chapter, the authors come to the interesting conclusion that having children does not add to the happiness of parents. In fact, they found a negative relationship between parenthood and life satisfaction in two-thirds of the countries surveyed. This negative effect is stronger in countries with higher GDP per capita or higher unemployment rates.

The report reiterated that happiness was the primary goal of public policy. It identified four national governments—Bhutan, Ecuador, UAE and Venezuela—which had appointed ministers for happiness responsible for coordinating their national efforts. The report concluded with the observation that the science of well-being was developing and will be crucial for advancing humanity by concentrating public policy on this.

As we have seen, the main objective of this report was to link happiness with multidimensional well-being like health, jobs. The central idea of this report was to link happiness data with SDGs.

World Happiness Report 2017

This report gave special attention to the social foundations of happiness for both individuals as well as nations. The top 10 countries remained the same as 2016 but there was shuffling of places between these countries with Norway attaining the first position followed closely by Denmark, Iceland and Switzerland.

On the basis of calculations, the report observed that bringing social foundations from the lowest levels to world average levels of 2014–16 would bring about significant increase in life evaluation.

The report pointed out that GDP in China had multiplied over five-fold over the past quarter century but the SWB for the same period fell before showing a recovery but the current levels were still, on an average, less than a quarter century ago. The data analysed for China showed a mark decline in SWB from 1990–2005 with substantial recovery after that. The unemployment situation as well as changes in social safety net that played a major role in explaining this phenomenon. The 1990s saw severe unemployment emerge in China with the social safety net breaking down. There was growing anxiety in people about job, income, security, family and health. Along with the growth in income there was a rise in material aspirations. Millions lost their jobs in state-owned enterprises.

Even if the unemployment rate decreased after 2004, employees who joined private companies lost the advantages they had previously received from the public sector, and those who stayed in the public sector discovered that new regulations eliminated lifetime benefits and guaranteed employment. This was the result of the government policy of restructuring state-owned enterprises many of which were inefficient and unprofitable.

In another chapter, the report explored why African countries lagged behind others in their evaluation of life. Despite many African countries becoming a democracy, the people have not become happier. Maybe it was because of disappointment with the kind of development taking place. Population pressures and poverty could also be factors explaining this. However, the authors of the chapter were confident about the future of Africa as they found that Africans were optimistic, which might enable them to live a happier life in the times to come.

In another chapter, the authors used surveys from the US, Australia, UK and Indonesia to find out the factors that were responsible for the considerable variables between individuals regarding happiness. Economic variables, social factors, health issues were taken into account. Interestingly, the authors found that in three Western societies diagnosed mental illness emerged as one of the most important factors. Depression and anxiety disorders were the main forms of mental illness which explained the variance of happiness in Western countries much more than factors like income. In fact, mental illness was a much more relevant factor than physical illness.

In another chapter, the authors tried to find out how role, work and employment impacted happiness in people and how the type of job and workplace environment affected subjective well-being. There was no doubt that people who have a job tend to evaluate their life more favourably than who are unemployed. Their data analysis showed that rising unemployment levels negatively affected everyone including those who were employed. They observed that those involved in manual labour were at a lower level of happiness. They also found that the workplace environment which includes work-life balance, autonomy, variety, job security, social capital, health and safety risks also influenced the level of life satisfaction.

Jeffrey D. Sachs in the chapter "Restoring American Happiness" showed how social foundation influenced the level of happiness in the United States. The study concluded that a decline in happiness among the Americans was primarily due to social rather than economic causes.

Norway, Denmark, Iceland, Switzerland and the Netherlands were among the top five countries in terms of happiness from 2014 to 2016. China was ranked 79th, whereas the US was ranked 14th. India once again fared poorly and was ranked 122nd.

This *WHR* should guide policymakers to realize that they must focus on developing social foundations if they want an increase in the level of happiness.

World Happiness Report 2018

The *WHR 2018* focused on happiness and migration in various parts of the world. It attempted to analyse whether those who migrated to other countries were able to provide better and happier lives to their families. The level of happiness also depended upon the extent to which migrants were accepted in the country to which they moved.

The incidence of migration was increasing with globalization. Not only was their happiness crucial, but so was the happiness of those they left behind in their home country and those who already resided at the destination. The study examined both international and rural–urban migration in relation to happiness.

Movement from rural to urban areas has been a worldwide phenomenon and was a consequence of the process of development. Migration increased with improvement in agriculture productivity and better employment opportunities elsewhere. The urban population had been increasing at a fast pace due to this migration. During the period 1990–2015, the urbanization percentage went up by 19 per cent with countries like China contributing to a 30 per cent increase. The number of people living in towns increased by over 1500 million people which was a result of natural population growth in cities as well as migration from villages.

According to the *World Migration Report* of 2008, the number of international migrants was 85 million in 1970 but rose to 244 million in 2015, which was an increase from 2.3 per cent of the world population to 3.3 per cent. The trends showed that there had been big migrations into North America and Europe from South/Central America, Asia and Africa. It was in the richer countries that the proportion of immigrants was high. Approximately 70 per cent of the population in countries like UAE and Kuwait constituted migrants. In 2015, the number of international migrants from different continents was 40 per cent from Asia and 30 per cent from South/Central America.

Quite a few of the international migrants (10 per cent) were refugees. It was undertaken to assess to what extent they were happy in the new destination. Two startling facts about immigrant happiness were found in the report:

1. The immigrants were roughly as content as the locals in a typical nation.
2. The happiness of each migrant was not dependent only on the happiness of locals. The degree to which locals welcomed immigrants also had a significant impact on how happy newcomers were.

The analysis showed that on an average migrants gain if they moved from a less happy country to a more happy one. But it was also discovered that not everyone who was relocating was happier. One reason was that they felt deprived in their new location when compared to wealthier people, and they were also cut off from their relatives and comfort zone.

Happiness of migrants was not affected by the number of years they spend in the new destination. They may experience an immediate gain in happiness, which reduced over time. Refugees were less happy than other migrants but then when the latter migrated they were also less happy than other migrants and so even they benefitted from moving to a new destination.

The issue of rural–urban migration was analysed in another chapter with special reference to China. Happiness of three groups of people was compared. The first group consisted of rural dwellers who remained in the countryside, the second group were the rural to urban migrants who were now living in towns and the third group consisted of those who had always been urban dwellers. It was found that even though the income level of the migrants had almost doubled by moving from the countryside, they were less happy than the people still living in rural areas. A possible reason could be that urban life was more insecure than life in the countryside and there was a lesser community feeling. The experience was mixed because the report found that in Thailand there was an increase in happiness due to migration but in South Africa there was a decline.

Those who were left behind got remittances from abroad which did improve their life satisfaction but there was also sadness, worry and anger which had a negative effect. The study found that there was no effect on the average happiness of the locally born. However, the local people were happier if the culture of the country was more accepting of immigrants. It was also been found that immigration could lead to local tension, which had political ramifications. For instance, the influx of refugees from Bangladesh and Myanmar to India has created a lot of political and local tensions. So was the case of refugees from Syria into European countries.

The report tried to find out to what extent migration is welcomed by the local population, and it came to the conclusion that moderate levels of immigrations were accepted better than rapid surges.

Secondly, the impact of unskilled immigration fell mainly on the unskilled people in the host country though they made a positive contribution also.

Thirdly, the attitude and the mindset of both the locals and the immigrants mattered immensely. Attitude of the former determined the extent to which the immigrants felt accepted. However, the report also said that there was a limit to which migrants could be happily absorbed in the country. One solution suggested was to try and raise the sending countries' level of happiness by providing them with financial assistance, helping them build institutions that would enable them to live better lives and enabling them establish their own degree of trust.

Once again, Finland with a score of 7.632 emerged as the happiest country followed by Norway, Denmark, Iceland and Switzerland. China was at the 86th position with a score of 5.246 and India languished behind at 133rd place with a happiness index of 4.190. The reason behind India scoring low was that the happiness index was based on a survey which took responses from people on whether they were "very happy", "quite happy", "not very happy" or "not at all happy" and a weighted rate of the responses was taken to calculate score. The Indian response could have been more on the side of not being very happy because of low per capita GDP, relative happiness as people aspired to have more amenities, corruption and a decline of social support with people moving from rural to urban areas.

As we have seen, this report focused on how migration experiences, displacement and economic mobility affect happiness.

World Happiness Report 2019

Every *WHR* focuses on different aspects of happiness. The *WHR 2019* explored the link between happiness and community. It went into the details of how people communicated and interacted with each other and how a feeling of being a member of a community could lead to greater happiness. According to the research, there was a strong link between the quality of life and how communities and its members engaged with one another.

This report analysed the happiness trends from 2005 through 2018 and tried to investigate what may have contributed to them. It also focused on evolution of happiness inequality. Happiness inequality is much more than income inequality. Often social inequality is more closely linked to subjective well-being. The inequality of happiness rose between 2006 and 2012 in western Europe and thereafter it had been falling steadily while in central and eastern Europe it had been falling faster. In the Commonwealth of Independent States (CIS) capital region, it had been stable, at first rising since 2013. In Latin America, it has been steady till 2014 and has risen since. While in most of Asia, the rise in inequality has been less.

While ranking of countries by happiness for the period 2016–18, the *WHR* attempted to show the six key variables to explain the scores. These include GDP per capita, social support, healthy life expectancy, freedom, generosity and absence of corruptions. Finland with a score of 7.769 topped the ranking followed by Denmark 7.600, Norway 7.554, Iceland 7.494 and Netherlands 7.488. China with a score of 5.191 was at the 93rd position while India fell further to the 140th rank with a score of 4.015. There was a large gap between the happiness level of the top 10 countries as compared to the bottom ones. In fact, the average life evaluations in the top 10 countries were more than twice as high as the bottom 10.

The report reiterated that the focus of public policy should move from GDP to more comprehensive measures of progress, particularly how people value their lives. It also suggested that there should be an increasing interest in understanding how government and institutional actions affect happiness and what policy changes could help people live happier lives.

According to the research, a good government is one that upholds an institutional framework that makes it possible for people to live better lives. It alluded to a 2019 report on global happiness and well-being policy that included surveys of happiness-oriented solutions in particular public policy domains, such as health or education. The quality of governance has four indicators—effectiveness, rule of law, quality of regulation and control of corruption which combine to form an index of quality of delivery. Then there are two indicators for voice and accountability and for political stability and absence of violence which combine to form an index of the democratic quality of government. As regard life evaluations, it was found that quality of delivery was more important than democracy variables. Countries which had been subjected to conflict had lower life evaluations. Such conflicts were evidence of bad governance.

Global population-weighted life assessments declined precipitously during the 2008–2009 financial crisis, but they recovered in 2011 before continuing to decline. The value was roughly at its post-crisis low in 2018.The falling pattern after 2011 was determined mainly by what was happening in the five countries with the largest population.

Interestingly, India showed a significant drop during this period. Global inequality of well-being had been fairly constant between countries while rising within countries. In terms of how life evaluation changed between 2005 and 2008 and 2016 and 2018, the majority of countries showed notable shifts in happiness levels; Benin was the biggest winner, while Venezuela and Syria were the worst losers. The degree of life happiness has been directly impacted by the quality of governmental policy delivery, particularly the management of corruption.

This report examined the relationships between voting behaviour of citizens and their level of subjective well-being. It has been found that the level of SWB has a direct influence on whether people vote in elections or engage in politics. Happy people are more likely to engage with the community but their level of political participation is a matter of study. A study in the report showed that if the people were satisfied with their lives they were more likely to vote. Though happy people were more likely to engage in politics, this relationship flattened at higher level of happiness. Regarding voting behaviour, it has been found that people were more likely to vote for the ruling party if their SWB level has improved. This acts as a powerful incentive for political parties in power to perform.

In order to stay in power, ruling political parties in India were increasingly emphasizing performance and raising the standard of living for the populace. The voting pattern in India also revealed that, while having lower levels of well-being, the poor and those who lived in rural areas recorded larger voting percentages than those who lived in urban areas.

This can be explained by the fact that the poor and the deprived sections perceived voting and political participation as a means of empowerment. The urban elite having attained a certain level of well-being exhibited political apathy. Issues like unemployment and inflation which adversely impacted SWB greatly influenced voting behaviour. Despite the emphasis on well-being, problems that caused emotional distress frequently played a significant role in elections in India. Happiness and incumbent voting were causally related. However the pattern differed from nation to nation.

Very often political parties resorted to populism because if people were unhappy, they vote for populists. In India, since there were still a large number of people who had low per capita income and lower levels of education and healthcare, they were more likely to respond to populist promises. Sometimes, these promises had an adverse impact on the financial health of the economy. The relative level of happiness in a country could also have an impact on the preference of people for populist politics. It also depended on the extent to which populist political movements had managed to tap into people's unhappiness. The *WHR* was of the opinion that there was a lot of scope to further research the relationship between SWB and voting behaviour.

The *WHR 2019* also studied the relationship between happiness and pro-social behaviour. Humans are an extremely pro-social species who get happiness out of helping each other and not only give their time but also money in order to help others. An increase in pro-social behaviour promoted happiness. Research showed that spending time helping was associated with emotional benefits for the giver. There was a positive relation between volunteering and SWB though experimental studies had shown that this relationship may be overestimated.

In contrast, the causal impact of financial generosity on happiness was supported by many studies. This was true even when the giver does not physically interact with the recipient. Thus, behaving generously could increase happiness of people. This was more so when people were free to choose whether or how to help, they were connected to the people they were helping and they could see how their help was making a difference. Policies and programmes that offered all these three ingredients are more likely to create greater happiness. Research also showed that the recipient of social behaviour also became happier as it led to positive emotions. Better public policy initiatives may result from fostering pro-social behaviour.

Finally, the *WHR* studied the state of happiness in the US and the role of digital media. It showed that since 2010, there has been a decline in the level of happiness and well-being among Americans. This has led to mental health problems in society despite improvements in economic parameters. The decline in social capital and social support and the increase in obesity and substance abuse could be responsible for this.

The report observed that there had been a greater intrusion of digital media into the lives of people, especially adolescents and this has led to lesser time for reading or sleeping and eventually a decline in happiness. Adolescents who spend more time on electronic devices were less happy than those who spent on other activities. Because people used digital media to compare their happiness to that of others, it also contributed to unhappiness. According to the *WHR*, in order to increase happiness, people and organizations should pay more attention to how people spend their free time.

The *WHR 2019* focuses on happiness and community, exploring how happiness has evolved over the past decade. The report highlights that the quality of life and happiness are influenced by how people connect with each other and their shared institutions, reflecting the rapidly changing social landscape.

World Happiness Report 2020

The *WHR 2020* focused on environment and its relationship with happiness. It considered the natural, social as well as urban environments. Every *WHR* comes with a new paradigm of happiness, which should be a concern of public policy. This *WHR* said that out of the six factors which explained happiness, four were related to social environment—having someone to count on, having a sense of freedom to make key life decisions, generosity and trust. It also dwelled on the impact of inequality on well-being. It was true that hardships were more prevalent among the poor people and a trusting social environment could provide greater support to these people in distress and lead to greater equality in well-being. The Nordic countries were ranked higher in happiness index because of a better social environment. Higher levels of social and institutional trust were critical in raising the level of happiness of the people and reducing inequality of well-being.

This report looked into the happiness of city life across countries and compared it with the happiness of those living in rural areas. The analysis reveals that city rankings and countryside rankings are almost identical. This is especially true for countries at lower levels of average national happiness. Those living in cities were happier than those living in rural areas. However, it was also true that the urban happiness was less and sometimes even negative in top-ranking countries. In fact, the average urban happiness tended to fall below the average rural happiness after some level of economic development. However, it was a fact that cities afforded a better economic environment and opportunity for diverse kinds of employments which do provide happiness to people. Despite this, rural population was happier than its urban counterpart in many richer countries. The main reason behind this was the sense of belonging to a community which people had in rural areas.

This was true even in the case of India which was not among the richer or the happier countries.

There was a strong sense of community, mutual assistance and trust in India's rural areas. On the other hand, city dwellers led solitary lives with minimal ties to the neighbourhood. Though city dwellers were happier than their rural counterparts due to the higher incomes, there was a greater degree of happiness inequality in metropolitan areas.

Sustainable economic development is essential for survival of mankind. For this, the report observed, there has to be a concern for protecting the natural environment. The inability to do could lead to higher levels of pollution with adverse impact on health and happiness. Trees, forests, lakes and gardens are essential for peace and happiness. The report tested the linkage between sustainable goals and life evaluations. They found that SDG 12 which related to responsible consumption and production and SDG 13 which related to climate action were negatively correlated with life evaluation. However, the report found that there was a positive correlation between international differences in life evaluations and achievements in attaining SDGs. In terms of happiness, there were increasing marginal returns which sustainable development gave.

Predictively, the top five countries were Finland (7.80), Denmark (7.64), Switzerland (7.560), Iceland (7.50) and Norway (7.44). India with a score of 3.573 was 144th out of 153 countries. In fact, the Indian score had gone down 1.2 points in 2019 as compared to 2015. The gap between the top and bottom countries remained large. The average life evaluations of the top 10 countries were twice as high as the bottom ten.

The report also found that strong social environments provided buffers against adversity. There were certain risks which had an effect on life evaluations. These risks include discrimination, ill health, unemployment, low income or loss of family support. For example, life evaluations for those with poor health were much lower than those enjoying good health. Similarly, a low trust environment pushed down the life evaluation score. Those who considered that they lived in a high trust environment feel that they were protected from risk factors or misfortunes. For every one of the identified risks to well-being, a stronger social environment provided significant buffering against loss of well-being, ranging from 30 per cent to over 70 per cent for the separate risks. The total effects of social environment were even greater when we added in the well-being benefits of personal social connections.

The report stated how rapid urbanization imposed a lot of challenges like lack of affordable housing, traffic congestion, pollution and crime in cities. It further observed that if cities strengthened the public transport system to reduce traffic congestion and commuting times, lowered ambient air pollution, and improved access to green and public open spaces for all citizens, they could provide better levels of average life satisfaction. The pressures of city life often led to worry, sadness and anger which made people unhappy. Things like availability of clean water, clean air, public infrastructure, housing affordability, jobs, climate, diversity and community attachment could lead to increasing the life evaluation of city dwellers. City life was quite unhappy for those who migrated from rural areas but lived in slums and were concerned with earning enough to maintain the daily necessities of life.

The global ranking of cities according to current life evaluation showed that the first five positions were attained by Helsinki (Finland), Aarhus (Denmark), Wellington (New Zealand), Zurich (Switzerland) and Copenhagen (Denmark) while the bottom five cities were Kabul (Afghanistan), Sanaa (Yemen), Gaza (Palestine), Port-Au-Prince (Haiti) and Juba (South Sudan). New Delhi was at the 180th position out of 186 countries.

The report noted that environmental concerns were becoming increasingly important when evaluating the quality of people's lives. Climate change in particular was garnering a lot of interest due to its potential effects on human existence itself. Increasingly it was being realized that green natural environment led to improvement in mental well-being, having an indirect positive impact by increasing certain behaviours like physical exercise. Green spaces provided clear health benefits, which contributed to a happier society. Stress was decreased and well-being was enhanced in a green, natural setting. According to the report, local environmental issues were more important in determining people's well-being than national environmental factors, which did not provide the best picture.

The *WHR* empirically explored the linkages between sustainable development and well-being. Each of the SDGs was evaluated to see its relationship with a sense of well-being. Once again it was found that countries with a higher SDG index score tended to do better in terms of SWB with the Nordic countries topping the list. There were increasing marginal returns to sustainable development in terms of human well-being. As already indicated, SDGs 12 and 13 were negatively correlated with subjective well-being. The report also studied other indices like human development index, index of economic freedom, global peace index, global competitiveness index, environmental protection index and GDP per capita. The report found that the SDG index and the other indices of development were positively and significantly corelated with subjective well-being. However, the relationship between SWB and the HDI was the strongest.

The report concluded by saying that there was an urgent need to combine the SDG and SWB research and policy agenda to generate solutions that work for both people and planet, and help accelerate sustainable development. There was also a study of why the Nordic countries were the happiest in the world. One of the main reasons for this was the welfare state model of development in which citizens were provided extensive social benefits. This had a positive impact on life evaluation.

The other reason was the quality of the governance and the satisfaction of the people with its performance. Good quality of public institutions also had a significant impact. The level of income inequality was also low. The people had a lot of trust in others and there was social cohesion. In addition, there was greater freedom to make life choices for individuals.

The report emphasizes the impact of urban living on life satisfaction and evaluations.

World Happiness Report 2021

The *WHR 2021* came after the pandemic which caused a great deal of unhappiness. The entire report focused on the effects of COVID-19 and the impact it had on the quality of lives of people and how they coped with this unforeseen catastrophe. Millions perished due to the virus. The report said that in 2020 there was a 4 per cent increase in the annual number of deaths over the previous year. People suffered from greater economic insecurity, anxiety, disruption in every aspect of life and the stress it caused was a great challenge to their mental and physical health.

Surprisingly, the report observed that people showed a lot of resilience in their responses to the survey on life evaluation. There was a change in the level of happiness as compared to the earlier years, but there was no significant change in the rankings. There was no overall change in the positive effect but the responses of the people showed that there was an increase in the number of people who felt sad or were worried. In this situation of a crisis it was the trust factor and the ability to count on others for support that assumed great importance. It was the trust factor that was important also in explaining the large international differences in the COVID-19 death rates. The confidence in public institutions was one of the important factors supporting successful COVID-19 strategy. Trusted public institutions were more likely to choose the right strategy and also get public support. The report also found that COVID-19 was better handled wherever the head of the government was a woman.

East Asia, Australia, New Zealand were success stories in handling COVID-19 in 2020. In these countries, citizens also complied with government policy and were more freedom-oriented. It was also found that morale of the people improved when the government took firm action. The countries with the highest number of deaths also had the greatest fall in GDP per capita. There was a close link between the health risk brought about by COVID and fall in GDP growth rate. There was a decline in the level of happiness as the confirmed cases of COVID increased. However, the strict mobility control and physical distancing policies considerably offset the decrease of happiness caused by rise in daily deaths. According to the research, Asia Pacific was far more successful in containing the pandemic than the North Atlantic region. This resulted from both top-down initiatives, where the government developed strict control policies, and bottom-up initiatives, where the population supported the government and complied with the regulations. The North Atlantic's success was negatively damaged by the region's individualistic culture and comparatively lax social norms. Lack of sufficient scientific knowledge among the population of the North Atlantic countries also contributed to their failure in effectively controlling the pandemic as people were vulnerable to false information and fake news.

The pandemic had a direct impact on the mental health of people worldwide especially women, the young and the poor. The pandemic exacerbated already existing inequalities in mental health.

However, the study found that after an initial sharp decline in mental health there was a considerable improvement in the average mental health but it did not come back to the pre-COVID level. The pandemic also disrupted mental health services. On the positive side, it made people more aware of mental health issues.

The strategy of physical distancing or self-isolation challenged social connection of people adversely impacting their happiness. Positive features like gratitude, grit, prior connections, volunteering, exercising and having a pet helped in maintaining the happiness level of people to a large extent. Digital connectivity also helped in promoting mental health of the people to a certain extent.

The report estimated that global GDP shrunk by roughly 5 per cent in 2020. Unemployment increased, in particular, people in low-income jobs were rendered jobless, causing a lot of misery to them. This was one of the greatest economic crises in a generation. Unemployment during the pandemic was found to be associated with a 12 per cent decline in life satisfaction and 9 per cent increase in negative impact. The happiness of the workplace was mixed with initial decline and then stabilization. Social support did protect people against the negative impact of unemployment. Work from home helped to a large extent in containing the negative impact of the pandemic.

India also suffered during the pandemic with an estimated 23 million people being pushed into poverty. The GDP growth rate for the year 2021 fell by almost 8 per cent.

The impact of this on the poor migrant labour was visible when they walked hundreds of miles back to their villages as they had lost their jobs and it was becoming difficult to meet the expenses of their daily life. The Indian government responded well by not having national-level lockdown after the initial one and tried to maintain a balance between the threat to life due to COVID-19 and livelihood.

In another chapter, the report says that to evaluate social progress and make effective policy one has to take into account the quality as well as the length of life. For this, the health economists used the concept of well-being adjusted life years (WELLBY). They found that WELLBY rose by 13 per cent between 2006–08 and 2017–19. There was a significant reduction in fundamental inequality which remained lower in 2020 despite COVID-19. Regarding public policy, the report said that it was difficult to use WELLBY approach due to lack of direct information about well-being. However, the science of happiness provided direct evidence and though the numbers may not be perfect they were adequate. Though public expenditure was a political decision, WELLBY provided a mechanism to direct it towards well-being.

In the ranking of countries by happiness based on 2020 surveys the situation was similar to earlier years. Finland, Denmark, Switzerland, Iceland and Netherlands remained the top five countries. The bottom five countries were Lesotho, Botswana, Rwanda, Zimbabwe and Afghanistan. India continued to have a very low rank of 139 out of 149 countries.

The main theme of this report was the impact of the pandemic on emotional well-being.

World Happiness Report 2022

The *WHR 2022* was released when the entire world was still reeling under the impact of the pandemic. It was the 10th anniversary edition of the report and began with an overview of the evolution of the concept of well-being over 10 years. It observed that most countries focused on progress of happiness of their people and that happiness could be measured. The national happiness rankings given in the report explored the trends over the past decade. The effect of the pandemic was also taken into account in the surveys. The science of happiness would guide the future progress and development policies in various countries. Interest in happiness and SWB showed a sharp rise and the attention to income and GDP was seen to be decreasing.

This report gives the rankings of the countries on happiness for the period 2019–21. The top five countries remained the same. The five countries at the bottom of the rankings were Botswana, Rwanda, Zimbabwe, Lebanon and Afghanistan. India dropped a couple of notches to the 136th position. Once again, the rankings showed a year-to-year consistency in the way people rate their lives. Finland continued to occupy the top slot for the fifth year in succession. However, many countries show a substantial difference in their scores due to the impact of the pandemic.

The data of 150 countries over 15 years showed how life evaluation and emotion have evolved over time. For example, life evaluation rose by more than a full point on a 0-10 scale in 15 countries but it fell by the same amount in eight others. Unfortunately, India is one of the countries which showed the largest drop. There has been a growth both in real GDP per capita and healthy life expectancy, fairly constant levels of social support, decline in perceived corruption, and substantial average growth in the extent to which people feel they have freedom to make key life choices and in helping strangers, and other forms of benevolence worldwide.

The life evaluations showed a great resilience during the pandemic though the level of stress went up. This was because frequency of positive emotions was twice as high as the negative ones. Though a large number of people became unemployed, there was an increase in trust and benevolence. The *WHR* revealed a bright light in dark times. The pandemic brought not only pain and suffering, but also an increase in social support and benevolence. As people battled the ills of disease, it became essential to remember the universal desire for happiness and the capacity of individuals to rally to each other's support in times of great need. And the people did just that. The trust factor was important in limiting the number of deaths due to COVID-19 as it meant that patients got timely treatment and psychological support. The report indicated a rise in the proportion of people engaging in charitable activities and helping others, reflecting a positive shift in social behaviour during crises around the world. According to the report, this outpouring of kindness provided grounds for hope and optimism in a world needing more of both.

The report examined the extent to which progress and well-being have evolved over time and how happiness became more relevant for policymakers. The word happiness has become more important in policy parlance and GDP has relatively declined in importance. People now talk of progress as being determined by going "beyond GDP". There was a growing realization that too much emphasis on GDP gave misleading indications to policymakers. The research on happiness was a global endeavour.

The report took into account the fact how increasingly social media platforms were being used by people to interact with each other, get information or entertainment. And how the pandemic exacerbated it. Social media had become the main source of communication between people. Research was being done on the language being used on social media to convey emotions including grief, rage and worry. According to the study, there was a significant rise in worry on social media at the beginning of the COVID-19 pandemic, which was linked to both the number of cases and the tightening of regulations.

The feelings of anxiety led to sadness and anger. In contrast to these three negative emotions, the expressions of positive emotions on Twitter during the first five weeks remained relatively stable. The analysis of social media during the pandemic revealed that social media data more accurately reflected the responses of the people in surveys for short-lived emotional experiences than longer-term well-being. Research indicated that emotions measured on social media can effectively track emotional contagion and user sentiments.

The report noted that well-being depended upon a lot of things. Apart from environmental influences, genetic factors were also critical in determining the well-being of people. The implication being that if you want to improve the level of well-being, personalized and diverse intervention would be required. Some people were found to be happier than others under similar circumstances. Genetic researches gave an answer to this. The report carried a study of twins which showed that identical twins had similar happiness ratings than fraternal twins. This indicated a strong influence of genetics on happiness. The interaction between genetics and environment determined the extent to which people were influenced by their environment. Some people were born with genetic variants that made it easier for them to feel happy. The individual's behaviour and happiness, driven by genetic makeup triggered environmental reactions. The level of sensitivity to the environment varies from person to person partly due to genetic differences. The study on twins in Europe showed that 40 per cent of individual differences in well-being could be explained by genetic factors.

The study concluded that there was no such thing as a single happiness gene. The overall genetic architecture of well-being was found to be polygenic, involving the cumulative effects of numerous genetic variants, each with small effects. It was clear that more research was required to understand the association between biological factors and well-being. The research would help in designing specific policy interventions to raise the happiness of people. It also showed that each individual was different and a policy could impact people differently.

Balance and harmony were closely linked concepts and had an association with the level of well-being in a culture. This aspect had not been studied in great detail so far. Balance means that the various elements which constitute a phenomenon and the various factors acting upon it are in proportionality and equilibrium, often with an implication of stability, evenness and poise. Harmony is used synonymously with balance at times but is slightly different. Harmony means that the various elements which constitute a phenomenon, and the various forces acting upon it, complement one another, leading to an overall configuration which is appraised positively. The report observed that inner harmony which comprised inner peace, contentment and balance was an important factor in determining the perception about happiness. Eastern philosophy and religion have laid more stress on balance and harmony as compared to Western thinking and culture.

In India particularly, almost all scriptures talk about the centrality of balance of harmony for a happy and successful life. The report found that the correlations between life evaluation and balance and peace are higher than between individual life evaluation and other variables which are determinants of happiness. The results of the study show that balance and harmony are closely related to the feeling of happiness all over the world. They are the core of well-being.

This report brought out the resilience of the family and the community in the time of the pandemic and how social support can contribute to life satisfaction even in the most difficult of times.

World Happiness Report 2023

The *WHR 2023* observed that national happiness was the most important objective for any government to achieve. This report brought out the consensus about how national happiness should be measured and the kind of behaviour that was required from individuals and institutions to achieve this. The report studied how the government can play a role in bringing about human happiness. It assessed how altruistic behaviours by individuals affect their own happiness as well as the overall happiness of society. Finally, the report examined and measured the level of happiness and distress through data available in social media.

The *WHR* talked about the happiness agenda for the next 10 years and was convinced that the best way of doing this was through a survey of people to find out how satisfied they were with their lives. If more people are healthy, prosperous and pro-social, the entire population is likely to experience a high level of satisfaction. The report was of the view that when we assess a society, situation or a policy we should not only look at the average happiness it brings but at the scale of low life satisfaction that might result. It contends that to prevent misery, governments and international organizations should establish rights such as those in the United Nation Universal Declaration of Human Rights. There should also be a focus on achieving SDGs to achieve happiness for future generations. Once happiness is accepted as the goal of the government, it is bound to have a profound effect on institutional practices.

Increasingly, policymakers have been talking about well-being. The OECD and the EU have called upon member governments to put people and their well-being at the heart of the policy design. According to the report, the central task of institutions was to promote behaviours and conditions of all kinds that are conducive to happiness. As a result of the evaluation of the responses to the millions of surveys done, the differences of well-being around the world both in and among countries were found to be mainly due to the following factors:

- Physical and mental health
- Human relationships (in the family, at work and in the community)
- Income and employment character virtues
- Social support including pro-sociality and trust
- Personal freedom
- Lack of corruption
- Effective government

The well-being of people depends upon social institutions and their performance in each country. The objective of every institution is to contribute to the development of human beings. Governments have to make the right policy choices to further well-being of their people.

NGOs also have a role to play in the well-being of people by their contribution to every sphere of human activity.

The report mentioned that much more needs to be spent on mental health and public health. Schools also have a positive role to play in the well-being of children as they inculcate value systems as well as life skills to students. Businesses too play a huge role in the generation of well-being as they supply customers with goods and services and provide employment. However, as Aristotle had once said, "Man is a social animal." Community life involving human connection was important in improving the quality of life of the people. The spectre of climate change dictates that society must focus on protecting the environment for present and future generations. The report emphasized the influence of the rule of law, the importance of family and individual belief systems of people on the well-being of the people.

The report indicated areas where more research was required. The relationship between virtue and happiness needed to be established. The link between policy and well-being using new tools and experimental methods was also required. Further subjective life evaluation needed a quantitative measure on which more work was required. The impact of well-being on other important outcomes, including longevity, productivity, pro-sociality, conflict, and voting behaviour, was to be investigated. The impact of social and political factors on well-being had to be thoroughly studied. However, one thing was clear that increasingly people were judging the state of affairs by looking at the level and distribution of well-being both within and across generations.

Life evaluations continued to be resilient with global averages in the pandemic years being just as high as those in pre-pandemic years. There is no doubt about inequality of happiness between countries and within countries. Countries having lower level of inequality of happiness were generally happier. The resilience could be explained by the trust and social support that were generated during the pandemic crises.

An analysis of data shows that for 2022, positive social connection and support were twice as prevalent as loneliness in key countries across the six global regions. This report continued to rely on three main well-being indicators of life evaluations, positive emotions and negative emotions to measure subjective well-being. Finland continued to occupy the top spot for the sixth year in a row with a significantly higher score than other countries. Denmark came second; Iceland was third, Israel occupied the fourth position while the fifth to eight positions were filled by the Netherlands, Sweden, Norway and Switzerland. This was the happiest Israel had ever been. The UK, by contrast, was ranked 19th, behind the US (15th). And the Israelites were even happier than the French (21st). For all its internal divisions and external conflicts, Israel was still a country driven by family and community connections to an extent that was (and still is) rare in the West. Even secular Israelis will have Friday night dinner together regularly and come together to celebrate festivals, Independence Day, births, bar and bat mitzvahs and huge weddings. There remains a large gap between the top and bottom countries. India was at the 126th position out of 137 countries with Afghanistan being at the bottom of the pile.

The major finding was that the effectiveness of government has a major role in determining the happiness of the people. The capacity of the state can be measured by looking at its physical capacity (ability to raise resources), its collective capacity (ability to deliver public services) and legal capacity (rule of law). The other crucial aspects being avoidance of civil war and repression. The report took these five measures of government functioning and correlated them with the average life satisfaction of people.

On the basis of these five characteristics, the states were classified into three clusters:

- common-interest states,
- special-interest states and
- weak states

In the common-interest state, the revenue was spent largely for the common good and the political institutions were sufficiently cohesive. There was a powerful incentive to invest in state capacity knowing future governments will continue to govern in the collective interest.

The special-interest state favoured the interest of a ruling group. State capacity in this case is primarily the state of the ruling group. Study also found that in those countries where life satisfaction was the highest it was also more equally distributed with fewer citizens having relatively low life satisfaction.

Weak states are those having low capacity to raise resources, deliver public services effectively and enforce rule of law.

It was found that the average life satisfaction in common-interest state was higher than in the other two states.

Despite it being obvious that governments should work towards the happiness of people, experience suggested that there were challenges in the way the governments could deliver this goal. Some states failed to provide effective social protection or build necessary infrastructure or ensure availability of services related to universal healthcare or basic education. In order to understand whether a government was able to pursue happiness as a goal of public policy it was necessary to appreciate the driving force behind the effectiveness of governments. The report identified two core dimensions of state effectiveness—ability to maintain peace and social order and build state capacity. The report observed that repressive regimes could enjoy short-term economic growth but in the long term they are not likely to succeed.

State capacity could support an effective state by strengthening the ability to identify and deliver efficient policy or by lowering their costs. The capacities of the state can be categorized as physical, legal and collective. These forms of state capacities were correlated across countries and were positively related to income per capita. The report concluded that peaceful states with larger state capacity were more conducive to higher well-being of its citizens. The conclusion was that there were a set of mutually occurring and reinforcing attributes of a state's performance that work together for the well-being of the citizens. Ultimately, to be effective, a state must move towards becoming a common-interest state with all of its positive attributes. An additional point was that it is the dispersion of life satisfaction across various sections of society and not just the level of life satisfaction that determined the effectiveness of a state.

There is an interesting chapter in this report which traces the relationship between doing good and feeling good, and the level of well-being. The report stated that altruism, which included helping strangers, donating money, giving blood and volunteering, led to greater happiness for both the altruist and the beneficiary. Experimental evidence showed that when the well-being of people increased, they became more altruistic. This report used data from social media to forecast the well-being of the population. The method has become more sophisticated since 2010. Social media data has become the largest cross sectional and longitudinal data set on emotions, cognitions and behaviours in human history. To use social media data to assess well-being is a cost-effective measure also. The report analysed how social media data could be used for evaluation of life satisfaction.

This report emphasized social support, trust and connectedness, and brought out that people's trust in government is a major factor influencing their happiness levels.

World Happiness Report 2024

The central theme of this report was that happiness varied according to different stages of the life of an individual and that happiness was shaped by both the life phase as well as social context. This report examined how happiness evolved from youth through adulthood to old age. It delved deep into the well-being of children and adolescents. It analysed global data in this category and discussed issues like education stress and social comparison.

This report tried to find out the relationship between happiness and aging as well as the rising cases of dementia risk in older populations. There is a complete chapter in this report analysing the differences in life satisfaction among older adults in India. Life satisfaction in older women was less than older men. It also found that older adults belonging to higher social castes reported higher life satisfaction as compared with those from Scheduled Caste and Scheduled Tribes. Adults with a higher-level of education were happier than those without formal education. The three top predictors of life satisfaction among older adults in India were living arrangements, perceived discrimination and health status. As regards the US and other Western countries, there were variations in the level of happiness of younger and older people.

As far as the ranking of countries is concerned, Finland and Nordic countries once again held the top positions. Sadly, India featured at the 126th positions out of 143.

The 2024 edition emphasized happiness across different stages of life, providing separate rankings for age groups for the first time.

World Happiness Report 2025

This *WHR* showed the deep linkage between life satisfaction and social connect. It observed that kindness, helping others and social ties were all manifestations of caring and sharing behaviour, which had a significant impact on happiness. Both the donors and the recipients gain by showing compassion.

Interestingly, the report finds that acts of kindness and supportive behaviour were increasing even after the pandemic. It took behaviour like returning lost wallets as a reflection of higher benevolence. Emotional well-being and life satisfaction were found to be substantially correlated with forms of care, such as social ties, supportive households and shared meals. The policy implication of this finding is that it is important to strengthen community networks, reduce social distress and encourage pro-social norms.

This report has established social behaviour and caring relationships as vital to happiness beyond the fulfilment of basic material needs. The 2024 and 2025 reports bring out that happiness is a multidimensional phenomenon shaped by structural, social and behavioural factors which have a far greater impact on happiness than GDP alone.

The world rankings on the happiness index once again follow a similar pattern with Finland maintaining the top spot for the eighth consecutive year. It has a high level of social support, trust, healthy life expectancy and freedom. The study also discovered that strong social ties and cultural factors that contributed to happiness and made nations like Costa Rica and Mexico rank highly. India improved somewhat from its 2024 ranking of 126th to 118th. The rating shows that, in comparison to other countries, India has difficulties with the social determinants of well-being. The 2025 report showed that happiness thrived where people cared for and shared with one another.

This research demonstrates how world happiness reports have progressed from the six fundamental elements of effective happiness to other determinants, with each edition concentrating on a new and pertinent facet of happiness, making the happiness index a genuinely multidimensional concept.

6

India's Poor Ranking in the Happiness Index

Why One of the Fastest-Growing Economies Is Unhappy

"The main message is that governments contribute to happiness or misery. Our national leaders seek wars. They should be trained in happiness before they blow us all up. The world must return to ancient wisdom."—Jeffrey D. Sachs

It is evident from the *WHR* reports for the past 10 years that the ranking of countries has been consistent. India's story is the same. India has been at the bottom of the ranking index in every *WHR*, and what is more concerning is that the ranking has declined with time.

To a certain extent, this is hard to understand and accept, but since each *WHR* has put India in a tough situation, it is necessary to discuss the specifics. India's policy planners should investigate the reasons behind the country's poor score. It is all the more surprising since many countries that are less developed than India and also some of them that are flawed democracies are ranked higher.

Is there a fault in methodology or sampling or just plain bias? Indian policymakers should diagnose the problem without which it would not be possible to design policies to improve the happiness quotient of its citizens. India was ranked 111th in the *2013 WHR*, but it has since dropped to a pitiful 139 in 2021 and 136 out of 146 in 2022. This is a dip of about 25 per cent which is surprising as India has been one of the fastest-growing economies in the world in the last few years. India's happiness ranking in the *WHR 2024* however improved to 126th out of 146 countries, remaining the same as the previous year. And in the *WHR 2025*, India ranked 118th out of 147 countries.

Why has India's ranking on the happiness index been declining?

India's enormous population and rapid population increase are major factors contributing to the country's low happiness index score. This leads to a lower rank in GDP per capita where India is at the 102nd position. As regards health, the Indian rank was 104 in 2021 which was a marginal improvement from 2018 when it was ranked 107th in this parameter. India's low ranking (141) in social support is unexpected because one would think that the country would do better in this area. Here is a comparison of India's rankings from 2018 to 2021 on a number of different criteria:

Table 6.1: World Happiness Report—India's Ranking

Year	2021	2020	2019	2018
Ranking of Happiness	139	144	140	133
Happiness score	3.82	3.57	4.02	4.19
Natural log of GDP per capita	102	102	103	103
Social support	141	145	142	144
Healthy life expectancy	104	104	105	107
Freedom to make life choices	31	37	41	56
Generosity	44	49	65	84
Ranking of positive effect	102	100	93	NA
Ranking of negative effect (reversed)	14	17	41	NA
Perception of corruption	75	79	76	84

Source: Samarth Jain, "Why India's ranking on happiness index has been falling" in *Governance Now* magazine, 9 June 2021

India is today one of the fastest-growing economies. Even for 2025–26 the growth rate is expected to be about

7.4 per cent which is among the highest in the world. The estimate for GDP growth for 2024–25 was also in the range of 6.5–7 per cent. Today, India is the fourth-largest economy in the world. In a few years, it is poised to leave Germany behind and become the third-largest economy in the world. When India achieves 100 years of freedom from colonial rule in 2047, it hopes to become a developed country.

However, the primary cause of India's appalling performance on the happiness index is its GDP per capita. India has continuously been ranked 102nd and 103rd in terms of GDP per capita, as Table 6.1 illustrates.

This is mostly because of the country's massive population, which stood at 1.41 billion (approximately 140 crore) in January 2026, even if the rate of population growth has significantly decreased. The per capita growth rate is significantly slowed by this enormous population. According to the IMF World Economic Outlook (October 2025), GDP (nominal) per capita of India in 2025 is projected at $2,818 at current prices. India is in 146th position out of 194 economies in terms of GDP (nominal) per capita. In 1993, India's GDP per capita was 6.49 per cent of the global GDP per capita; it improved to 19.4 per cent in 2025.

Inequality

Daniel Kahneman, the Nobel Prize-winning economist, recently conducted research on the Happiness Plateau, which determines how much money a person needs to be happy. His research on the US showed that the plateau has increased six times, from about $75,000 in 2010 to $500,000 in 2021. Above the threshold level of $500,000, money ceases to matter for happiness. This means that money continues to be the most important determinant of happiness as most people would be earning less than this amount. Finland has a per capita income of around $56,000 in purchasing power parity terms.

This result is also different from the original research of Kahneman which argued for the importance of non-economic factors of well-being. However, in the case of India the relationship between happiness and income is very close because the per capita income is so low. Additionally, there is a great deal of disparity in society; since 1940, the income of the bottom 50 per cent of people has dropped by almost 40 per cent. On the other hand, since 1980, the top 1 per cent's portion of the national income has grown by over 180 per cent, while the top 10 per cent's share has expanded by around 80 per cent. When compared to other emerging countries, India has had the largest increase in relative income disparity.

At the same time, consumption spending inequality has been decreasing, with poorer households experiencing faster increase. Every group's average consumption expenditure has decreased during the pandemic. The country's high rate of poverty is the primary cause of this. Lower levels of well-being are explained by characteristics such as caste, gender and family background disparity in addition to economic inequality.

The availability of school facilities, sanitation and basic infrastructure like electricity, water or healthcare are all examples of this inequality. Crime rates are on the higher side because of social and economic factors and the large population poses greater risks to environmental damage. The most painful thing is opportunity disparity, particularly in this day and age when, thanks to social media and television, individuals are aware of the standard of living that others in society enjoy.

Social justice

Caste discrimination is specific to Indian society and persists despite advancements and changes over time. There has been political empowerment of the backward castes and India today is a vibrant democracy; however, not all have gained equally through the democratic process. Much more needs to be done to uplift all castes and eliminate caste discrimination. Until this is accomplished, it will continue to be a significant contributing cause to India's low level of happiness.

Generosity

Table 6.1 shows that India has performed well in terms of generosity, with its happiness index ranking rising from 84th in 2018 to 44th in 2021. Indians are generally aware of their social responsibility and religiously inclined towards charity and helping others. In fact, Indians believe that everything should be done to make a guest feel comfortable even at the cost of personal discomfort. India should have ranked even higher on this metric, but the low per capita income acts as a dampener once more.

Social support

Mutual trust, sharing and caring for one another are examples of social support, which is frequently the most significant non-economic factor contributing to happiness. Surprisingly, India's ranking on this happiness index criteria dropped from 144th in 2018 to 141st in 2021, placing it near the bottom of the index. This perhaps accounts for the fact that the overall happiness score of India has declined from 4.19 in 2018 to 3.82 in 2021 and the ranking has come down from 133rd in 2018 to 139th in 2021 (Table 6.1).

The Indian government spends a lot of money in giving subsidies and pensions to disadvantaged groups and there are numerous development schemes targeted at improving the quality of life of the poor and this should count as a positive in social support. However, this indicator, perhaps, is more concerned with the support that people in society provide to one another. It is something which needs to be studied in detail.

Healthcare

In terms of healthy life expectancy, it was ranked 104th in 2021 and that has essentially remained unchanged. The reason has been low public expenditure in India which is at 1.3 per cent of GDP currently. This needs to be doubled at the earliest if we want to improve the quality of healthcare. There is an acute shortage of doctors, nurses and paramedical staff. Efforts are being made by the government to open more medical colleges and nursing institutions but the impact of this will be felt after some years.

In India, out-of-pocket medical expenses are quite high, ranging from 60 to 65 per cent. This means that the poor and lower middle class spend a significant amount of their income on medical treatment, which contributes significantly to their lack of wellness.

It is obvious that public expenditure needs to significantly improve in terms of both quantity and quality. The private sector also needs to be encouraged to expand and provide quality healthcare at affordable costs. Nowadays, private healthcare is so expensive that it is out of reach of most people. District hospitals are inefficiently managed and lack specialists, equipment and medicines. Primary health centres suffer from absence of doctors and medical staff.

The answer may lie in digitization of healthcare and telemedicine. Infant mortality rates in India are still very much on the higher side though there has been an improvement in maternal mortality rates. The scourge of diseases like TB and encephalitis still looms over the horizon. India has a severe malnutrition problem, with a high rate of childhood stunting and wasting. In addition, there is inadequate and poor quality of water availability and low standard of hygiene and sanitation. All of these account for a lower healthy life expectancy in India.

Freedom to make life choices

From 56th in 2018 to 31st in 2021, India's ranking improved on the indicator of freedom to make life choices. This is a sign of the nation's thriving democracy. Furthermore, it demonstrates that people's consciousness and educational levels have increased, enabling them to make decisions in life.

Corruption

The stance on corruption is worrisome. People in India perceive the government as corrupt and on the corruption index it is very much on the negative side. In fact, many writers have said that on the basis of a survey India emerges as the most corrupt country in Asia. Technology has the potential to revolutionize everything, and both the Indian government and state governments have made e-governance a top priority. Systemic reforms like greater transparency, more competition, changes in police and judiciary, and harsher penalties are required. Since corruption starts at the top, India must eliminate it from its electoral process in order to improve public perception. In terms of intangible criteria like happiness, laughter and enjoyment, India was better than many of its neighbouring countries but still ranked 102nd in 2021. However, India performed poorly and its ranking declined between 2018 and 2021 when it came to negative effects as determined by variables like unhappiness, worry and rage.

Table 6.2: Comparative Ranking of India and Her Neighbours on the World Happiness Index (2021)

WHR 2021	**India**	**Pakistan**	**Bangladesh**	**Nepal**	**Sri Lanka**
Ranking of Happiness	139	105	101	87	129
Happiness score	3.82	4.93	5.03	5.27	4.33
Natural log of GDP per capita	102	111	112	117	76
Social support	141	133	126	105	80
Healthy life expectancy	104	113	88	93	61
Freedom to make life choices	31	108	39	83	59
Generosity	44	49	102	38	36
Ranking of positive effect	102	132	138	139	21

Source: *WHR 2021*

As Table 6.2 shows, compared to its neighbours, India has not performed well in the happiness index. The 105th rank of Pakistan, the 101st rank of Bangladesh, the 87th rank of

Nepal and the 129th rank of Sri Lanka contrast negatively with India's ranking of 139. It is hard to accept that Pakistan is happier than India, and this raises legitimate concerns about the process used to determine the happiness index rankings.

The level of economic development of India is definitely far ahead of Pakistan, Nepal and even Bangladesh. I am sure the quality of life in India is much better. Although Sri Lanka's social metrics have improved, the country has experienced a period of civil war and government repression that cannot be conducive to increased happiness.

A closer analysis of India's ranking as compared to her neighbours shows that there is a vast difference in happiness scores. India's score is 3.82 but Pakistan's score is significantly higher at 4.93, Bangladesh is at 5.03, Nepal is at 5.27 and Sri Lanka at 4.33. The GDP per capita ranking of India at 102 is superior to Pakistan, Bangladesh and Nepal but less than Sri Lanka. If we look at Table 6.2, we find that India is performing better than Pakistan in per capita income, healthy life expectancy, generosity, freedom to make life choices and ranking of positive effects.

It is hard to understand why India stands more than 34 places behind Pakistan in the happiness index. Similarly, Sri Lanka is behind Pakistan, Bangladesh and Nepal despite being far ahead in GDP per capita, social support, healthy life expectancy and ranking of positive effect. The *WHR* report from 2021 provided an explanation of the ranking system. According to the report, rankings are solely based on respondents' average life assessments from Gallup surveys. The surveyors' efforts to connect these criteria with life evaluations are reflected in Table 6.2, which lists the six factors utilized for life evaluation.

Nevertheless, there is one last factor with two components that is not included in this table. The first is the residual error, which is the portion of the national average that cannot be explained by the *WHR* model. The second is the estimated life assessment in the imaginary nation of Dystopia, whose anticipated life evaluation (2.43) is determined using the lowest observed values for each of the six variables worldwide. Rankings are based on the average life evaluation, which is the total of all factors when dystopia and the residual are taken into account.

Table 6.3: Happiness Rankings of the BRICS Nations

Country	Happiness	Rank
Brazil	6.33	35
Russia	5.477	76
India	3.82	139
China	5.33	84
South Africa	4.956	103

Source: *WHR 2021*

Among the BRICS nations, India is ranked lowest in the happiness index as shown in Table 6.3.With the exception of GDP per capita—which is calculated using purchasing power parity adjusted to a constant of 2011 international dollars from the World Bank's World Development Indicators report, and healthy life expectancy at birth, which is derived from WHO data—the predictors in the table are primarily based on answers to Gallup Poll survey questions. The GWP asked the following question about social support: "If you were in difficulty, do you have family or friends you can count on to aid you whenever you need them or not?

The national average of answers to the GWP question, "Are you satisfied or dissatisfied with your freedom to choose what you do with your life?" is used to calculate the fourth parameter of freedom to choose life choices. Generosity figure is arrived at by taking the residual of regressing the national average of GWP responses to the question "have you donated money to a charity in the past month?" on GDP per capita.

The average of binary responses to two GWP questions—"Is corruption widespread throughout the government or not?" and "Is corruption widespread within business or not?"—is used to determine how corruption is perceived.

Positive effect is defined as the average of previous-day effect measures for happiness, laughter and enjoyment. The negative effect is defined as the average of previous-day effect measures for worry, sadness and anger. To comprehend India's poor ranking in the happiness index, it is necessary to examine the answers that Indians provided to the GWP questions as well as the effects of the residual elements. I am not sure if the high aspirations of the youth and desire to advance in life could encourage them to provide negative replies to

GWP questions, which would result in a bad score for the country.

Having said that, I do not believe that policymakers in India should ignore its low ranking on the happiness index. A proper diagnosis of this lack of well-being should be done because India is a welfare state and should target optimal amount of happiness for its people.

Policy prescription to make India happy

By 2047, India hopes to be a developed country. Ajay Chibber, distinguished scholar at George Washington University and former assistant secretary general at the UN, has created a roadmap that would make India a happy nation. He says that India must reach an average yearly per capita level of $12,500 by 2047 to move from middle-income status to higher-income status. By 2047, India hopes to have an economy worth between $25 and $30 trillion, making it a superpower.

India is likely to become the third-largest economy in the world in the near future, but Chibber believes that this is unlikely due to the country's extreme economic inequality. According to him, India is stuck in a middle-income trap, and needs to be reimagined and reshaped if it wants to become not only more prosperous but a happy nation. It has to become more inclusive, democratic and sustainable, and provide a better life for its women and marginalized communities. It must develop into a caring society that encourages innovation, creativity and initiative.

Structure of governance

For India to be happy it must ensure that the sanctity of the institution of democracy is not only preserved but strengthened. India's objective of social, economic and political justice empowerment is embodied in its beautiful Constitution. The spirit of the Constitution must prevail at all levels of governance. The fundamental framework of the Indian Constitution must remain inviolable. India should uphold social harmony, peace and unity at all costs. It should aim for upliftment of all sections of society.

India benefits greatly from a large demographic dividend, but in order to capitalize on this, it must prioritize educating its children and giving all its boys and girls equitable access to high-quality education. Additionally, the state needs to develop a network of policies to manage the vital field of healthcare and give everyone access to the bare minimum of medical facilities. The nation should concentrate on making significant improvements to its infrastructure for health and education. Public health and education have to be the focus areas for the government along with internal security, defence, water and sanitation, and other public goods.

The Indian populace would be happier if the government does not intervene in every aspect of life. To help people reach their full potential, it is important to support their personal initiatives and inventiveness. This calls for an approach that combines maximum governance with minimum government. Decentralization and delegation should be implemented at all administrative levels. Local self-governments, which must be democratic and reinforced by the delegation of funds, personnel and functions, should handle local matters. In the economic sphere the government should play the role of a facilitator and regulator rather than be an actor. This would inflame the primal instincts of the economy.

To fight against corruption, several measures have been taken, including the introduction of technology, building systems and developing an institutional framework. Yet, the perception about corruption in India remains high. A significant contributing element to India's declining ranking in the happiness index is the common Indian citizen's complaints about government corruption in relation to his daily life.

The problem is not likely to be wished away but a combination of systemic reforms, greater transparency, greater competition and a greater use of IT-based services would help in curbing this problem. Honesty should be rewarded by the system. Instead of what appears to be the case now, corruption ought to be viewed as a high-risk, low-return endeavour.

Regional disparities

India has enormous regional differences in social and economic growth, and the government must step in to help those states and districts that are falling behind. Perhaps a beginning in the right direction is the recent effort to classify the majority of backward districts as aspirational districts and backward blocks as aspirational blocks. To achieve balanced regional development, planning for development should be done at the village level rather than being forced from above.

India must develop an institutional system to guarantee that the SDG targets are accomplished within the allotted time frame by 2030. In particular, India must focus on eradicating absolute poverty and hunger by that year.

Role of women

Much more needs to be done to improve the lot of women in the country. A recent study has shown that the current labour force participation rate of women in India is barely 35.3 per cent as of December 2025, which is abysmally low, and even a few percentage-point increase in this will have a sizeable impact on the growth rate of the country. Women's safety and protection from sexual exploitation and gender-based violence must be the top priorities. The law and order apparatus must be strengthened so that women are able to roam around freely, even at night, without fear of being molested.

Women need to be educated and made aware so that they can participate in the political, economic, social and family life on an equal footing. The government must provide high-quality education to the girl child from elementary school to postgraduate level. All socioeconomic indices, including the rate of newborns and maternal deaths as well as the degree of malnutrition in children and pregnant women, would significantly improve as a result of this alone. This should help in reducing the gender imbalance in India.

Political empowerment is absolutely essential and the recent move to have 33 per cent reservation for women in parliament is a laudable one. Equal representation of women should be encouraged in all top management and administrative posts. A policy framework must evolve which helps women entering the jobs stream. There should be more female students enrolled in management, scientific, and engineering programs. Fortunately, this is already happening with the current figure being around 43 per cent.

Agriculture

The backbone of the Indian economy is the farmer. Agriculture employs 45 per cent of the nation's labour force although it contributes only 15 per cent of GDP. The farmer in India is facing a lot of economic distress. This is true even though farmers receive substantial subsidies for fertilizer, seeds, water fees and electricity expenses. The main reason is that the agriculture marketing system operates in a manner that is not beneficial to the farmer.

There is a working minimum support price (MSP) system for wheat, rice and cotton although only a few states can benefit from it. In the rest of the country, farmers have to face the market system and are not strong enough to get positive terms of trade. It is clear that major structural reforms are required in agricultural marketing so that farmers can get a remunerative price for their produce. The problem of fragmentation has become endemic and a policy framework is required to bring farmers together. For this to happen, farmer producer companies or organizations have to be formed and empowered.

Manufacturing and services

India would be a happier country if workers can move from farm occupations to non-farms ones. It is crucial to enhance agriculture by establishing a network of food processing businesses, ideally in the rural hinterland. The share of manufacturing sector in the economy must go up so that more employment is generated in this sector. Startups need to be encouraged particularly in IT services, healthcare and agriculture. India must become a leader in IT rather than being just a back office. Policymakers should pay attention to India's enormous unrealized tourism potential and the huge employment it creates.

Sustainable development has to be the motto. India is a developing economy and cannot completely avoid fossil fuels but there has to be a plan for the transition to clean energy. If a suitable policy solution is not developed, climate change will negatively affect India's growth narrative. We must do everything in our power to drastically cut down on air and water pollution and improve the quality of life in cities and villages.

India is undoubtedly a unique case for study of national and individual happiness because it is a diverse country and has had a long history of foreign invasions. It has the largest concentration of Hindus in the world and a sizable population of Muslims and Christians. India is a bundle of contradictions. Rapid economic growth is occurring on the one hand, while extreme poverty and malnutrition exist on the other. It is developing at a rapid pace but this growth is not leading to a required level of employment, which makes the nation's youth unhappy.

Robert Biswas-Diener, Louis Tay and Ed Diener in the book *Happiness across Cultures* provide a thorough analysis of happiness in India. The authors make an interesting observation that happiness in India is both and "inside-out" as well as "outside-in" phenomenon. This suggests that while internal, personal factors account for a significant portion of an individual's pleasure, external, material circumstances also have an impact.

The authors recommend that the government could maximize the happiness of its citizens by promoting economic, labour and healthcare policies to improve collective well-being. They claim that in addition to enhancing inner happiness, citizens should participate in awareness-raising initiatives that teach people how to set goals and appreciate happy times.

Data effect on Indian ranking

One of the reasons why the ranking of India in happiness index has been relatively constant at a low level is that much of the data was collected before India entered the phase of rapid economic growth which was visible only after 2004–05. Indians were given questions about a wide range of topics in the Gallup global survey, from having running water at home to being content with one's own health. According to the 2007 Gallup Poll, India scored lower than the global average on the labour index (India: 24; global average: 30) and the food and shelter index (India: 64; global average: 75).

However, India ranked exactly at the world average for the health index and slightly above on the law and order index. India reported fewer positive emotions and more negative emotions. The authors had studied both the economic and cultural basis of happiness in India. Though their analysis may be not so relevant as it was done in 2012 and based on data at that time, it does suggest some interesting aspects of how Indians look at happiness.

According to the authors' analysis of the Gallop poll at the time, India's happiness index is low when compared to other nations but survey participants reported absolute levels of happiness in the positive range. This means that India cannot truly be described as an unhappy nation and it is possible that people are generally happier than their GDP per capita indicates.

There are disparities in the degree of happiness between rural and urban areas of India. India's life evaluation score for 2012 was 5.20, with rural India scoring 4.98 and urban India scoring 5.24. Similarly, India's total positive sentiment score was 0.70, with rural India reporting 0.68 and urban India 0.73. This implies that urban dwellers are happier than rural residents. The data does support this, but if you look at the quality of life in rural and urban India, you will see that there is a lot of poverty in urban areas, with many people living in slums and on the streets and having little to no access to the necessities of a good life. Furthermore, polls have consistently demonstrated that social support is a key component of happiness, and in this sense, I believe that rural Indians are far happier than urban Indians. While people in urban India experience a great deal of alienation and loneliness, in rural India the community is one and there is a lot of sharing and closeness.

It is also a fact that happiness index is calculated on aggregated happiness data which gives a general picture of happiness but does not indicate anything about the individual or smaller groups. Policymakers in India must conduct national polls that fully understand the phenomenon. We could compare data on people's levels of happiness in India with samples from Bangladesh, a country with a comparable culture to India. Brinkerhoff (1997) found that 55 per cent of the residents of one Indian Himalayan village and 62 per cent of the residents of the other village were content with their lifestyles in a research on happiness in India utilizing smaller Indian samples. Despite the difficulties of living in a village, only 4 per cent of people in the first village and 9 per cent in the second expressed active dissatisfaction. Similarly, researchers have discovered that Indian slumdwellers showed a moderate level of pleasure with their life despite living in extremely poor economic situations.

Though shortage of quality housing and low-income level were important but family satisfaction was equally relevant. For most Indians living in poverty, the society provides local protective factors to shield them from the negative effects of poverty. The social fabric of Indian lives is, in fact, a source of happiness, according to the authors' analysis of the Gallup Poll data.

The above are the outside-in factors but the inside-out factors are more relevant in India. Culture and national happiness are closely related since cultural elements affect how people feel and behave. There are different ways of looking at life in India as compared to the Western world. For example, pride is viewed badly in the Indian ethos, although it is positive in Western civilization.

The majority of Indians believe in the notion of karma, which has greatly contributed to fatalistic thinking and the idea that a person's current fate is determined by his deeds in a previous life. An Indian is therefore more inclined to accept situations since he thinks they are beyond his own control.

Policy interventions can address the outside-in variables, but the inside-out elements must be taken into account too. Therefore, it is crucial that policymakers consider both subjective aspects of well-being and economic metrics. Material, social and spiritual fulfilment are all equally significant in India's comprehensive conception of pleasure.

India must therefore comprehend the reasons behind the unhappiness of its people and take a comprehensive strategy to development in order for every segment of society to advance and experience a significantly higher standard of living.

Indian studies on happiness

Survey conducted by Rajesh Pillania

There have been some other surveys also that present different pictures about happiness in India. In 2020, a India happiness report was released covering 28 states and eight union territories. Dr Rajesh Pillania, a professor of strategy at the Management Development Institute in Gurugram, wrote the paper. From March to July 2020, a sample of 16,950 individuals across states and union territories participated in the survey. The conclusion was that the happiness rankings of Mizoram and Andaman and Nicobar Islands are the highest. Among the big states, Punjab, Gujarat, Telangana occupy the top three positions. Oddly, this report finds that people of Uttar Pradesh are happier than those in Maharashtra and Tamil Nadu.

With Mizoram at the top with a score of 3.57 and Chhattisgarh at the bottom with a score of 3.19, none of the states appear to have scored very high on the happiness index. The happiness scores of the different states do not significantly differ from one another. The study's findings also indicated that while marital status, age group, income level and education are all positively correlated with happiness, there is no significant association between gender and happiness.

While the results of various surveys may differ, one thing is certain: public policy must prioritize happiness.

It is undeniable that there are some issues that require the government's attention, even though we in India may not agree with the results of global happiness reports on our country. The welfare of the populace must be closely considered when formulating policy.

India Today's study on happiness (2016)

In a special edition published on 16 January 2016, *India Today* magazine examined the key to happiness with a focus on India. The magazine's articles voice alarm over India's persistently low standing in global happiness surveys. This is true even though Indians have a reputation for being content under the most trying circumstances. It also highlights the fact that, despite the Nordic countries' high scores on the World Happiness Index, an internal survey conducted in 2018 revealed that mental illness and loneliness are prevalent in these nations, with Sweden having the highest suicide rate and Finland having it as the third leading cause of death for those aged 16 to 24.

Survey conducted by HappyPlus Consulting (2023)

In 2023, an Indian business called HappyPlus Consulting conducted a thorough survey in India, covering various mental and emotional well-being aspects, and asserted that its sample size was significantly larger than that of the polls used in the world happiness report. They arrived at a life evaluation score of 6.84 for India, which is nearly twice as high as what the *WHR* has reported. According to this poll, the happiest states in India were Himachal Pradesh, Punjab, Uttarakhand, Kerala, Maharashtra, Tamil Nadu, Puducherry and Goa. Uttar Pradesh is at the bottom of the list. With Chandigarh and Delhi being the happiest union territories.

According to their survey, 87.8 per cent of Indians believe they have social support and can safeguard their mental health in the face of adversity, which results in a happier mood and pro-social behaviour. Additionally, it discovered that as people in India age past 25, their level of life satisfaction declines. However, people report increased levels of satisfaction as they age, particularly around sixty. According to the survey, India's general level of happiness can be regarded as moderate.

The widespread belief among Indians that the government is corrupt is one of the things that lowers their level of happiness. According to the survey, 43.2 per cent of Indians think that corruption is pervasive in both business and government. Additionally, it reports that 32.9 per cent of Indians experience negative emotions including worry, despair and anger on a regular basis. Individual satisfaction and the nation's advancements in the social, economic and environmental spheres are related.

The report observed that 65 per cent of Indians experience anxiety and stress on a regular basis due to health and financial concerns, issues with friends and family, and pressure at the workplace. Higher awareness of emotional well-being and taking constructive action to advance in life are two ways to address this.

In a study of SWB indicators, such as life evaluations, positive and negative emotions, freedom to choose, perception of corruption, state-level per capita, net domestic products, consumer price index, literacy rate, healthy life expectancy at birth, multidimensional poverty index and health index, it was discovered that women and men have different levels of happiness. Women are more likely than men to express happiness and laugh, but they also experience higher levels of worry, sadness and anger.

The level of negative emotions increased for both men and women due to COVID-19. Maharashtra, Delhi and Haryana were most negatively impacted by COVID-19.

The Week *magazine's study on happiness (2023)*

What makes Finland the happiest place on earth?

In its 23 April 2023 issue, *Week* magazine attempted to determine why Finland was the happiest nation on earth. This indicates that the pursuit of happiness is becoming a major topic for Indians who want to research and assess in order to find a way to achieve happiness in the future.

Love of nature

The magazine included a cover story explaining why Finland had been named the happiest nation for six years running, not just in 2023. It observed that happiness is a journey not a destination, but it seemed to be the destination for most people. Finland is home to 56 lakh people, known for its long, dark and cold winters. Summer is beautiful but it also gives birth to large size mosquitoes. According to their philosopher Frank Martela, the Finnish were doubtful of their rating since it does not align with their perception of themselves as serene, reclusive and even depressed. In general, Finns seemed gloomy and did not tend to converse too much. What exactly made the Finns happy? It seemed they enjoyed the small pleasures of life, like vacationing with their family and friends in summer cottages. There were 32 lakh cottages and most of them are near clear lakes in forests.

In fact, 80 per cent of Finland was forest. Summer holidays were about living a simple, rustic life communing with nature. The Finns found great joy in spending time in nature and enjoyed the quiet that lay beneath the city's cacophony and worries. The happiness came from living a quiet life of hiking in pristine forests, picking berries, plucking mushrooms, fishing in rivers, chopping wood, kindling fire, playing outdoor games and barbecuing.

The sauna is a favourite pastime of the Finns because it heated their icy bones and warmed their souls. It is an intangible aspect of Finnish culture and a place for introspection, cleansing and socializing. The sauna is to the Finns what the church is to Christians.

Contentment

As we have seen, happiness is a relative concept and frequently a transient feeling of contentment with life.

The Finnish sense of well-being is routed in strong social support from family, friends and government. People have a decent quality of life because of the high per capita GDP levels. The majority of Finns enjoy civic comfort and are homeowners.

Like the other Nordic nations, Finland is a social democracy with shared and equitable wealth. From birth to death, the state looks after its residents. There is no feeling of job uncertainty. Everyone has access to high-quality, free education, ensuring that everyone has equal opportunities. Citizens have good health, civic virtue and good habits, and their basic requirements are satisfied. A primary objective of public policy is well-being, and the happiness surveys indicated that well-being played a more significant role in explaining election outcomes than the economy. Stable governments have taken office in Finland through elections, and despite coalitions of several different parties, the government functioned well.

Homogenous society

Anita Pratap, the author of the *Week* piece, expressed surprise that Finland was the happiest country in spite of its violent past. Finish nationalism was cemented by a homogenous society. There were fewer immigrants in Finland compared to the other Scandinavian countries.

When it came to civic integrity, cleanliness, modesty and trust, Finns scored highly. They did not flaunt their affluence. The Finish language united them as a tight-knit community. Pratap was conscious of the negative aspects of Finnish living that contributed to the country's high suicide rate. One explanation, according to her, would be the long, gloomy winter that caused sun deprivation, which lowered the body's neurochemical levels. Another issue was alcoholism.

Resilience

The Finns think that life should be lived now rather than waiting for better times. They have the courage to stand up to adversity.

They display the ability to overcome the extreme cold weather conditions with grit and determination. The Finland story is about creating trustworthy, responsible, citizen-focused institutions to meet people's basic needs. Their balanced lifestyle is one factor contributing to their contentment. They don't have a brutally competitive culture. They are a civilization seeking a decent and balanced life rather than one with limitless desires.

Trust in government

In Finland, free education, healthcare, income security and pensions are guaranteed to everyone. Democratic governance, efficient public services and human rights are prioritized. The Finns believe in honesty and equality. The people trust the government and are confident that it will take care of them in adverse times, and the government deliver on these expectations. Effective governments are thought to be the least corrupt. The government has a high degree of accountability. The society focuses on gender equality, social justice, work-life balance and human development. The government spend heavily on social areas to provide good quality of life to its citizens. Crime rates are low and there is a high level of public safety. The citizens trust each other and the authorities. Because the government is accountable and corruption is minimal, individuals are also prepared to pay high taxes in exchange for benefits that last a lifetime.

Role of institutions

Frank Martela, in a guest column of the same magazine, observed that the high-quality institutions were responsible for the high rankings of all Nordic countries on the happiness index. These institutions served as watchdogs for democracy, corruption and press freedom. Furthermore, the high happiness rankings were a result of these nations' welfare systems. Many reasons of sadness were eliminated from people's lives by well-run organizations and welfare services.

Martela was of the view that the rise of citizen happiness should be celebrated while a drop in average happiness should be treated like a national crisis. In his words, the ultimate secret to Finnish happiness was the fact that institutions were accountable to citizens at large and not just serving narrow elites within it.

With a GDP per capita (purchasing power parity) of $48, 631, Finland was ranked 17th in the world. In terms of the proportion of people living below the poverty line, Finland was ranked second with a ratio of 0.057. Air pollution exposure was the lowest in the world, while health spending per capita ranked 18th in the world at $3640.10. Finland ranked fourth in the world for social spending, allocating 29.02 per cent of its GDP to this sector.

Finland ranked 16th in terms of education spending, which was high at $18, 128 per student. The most significant finding was that the respondents' level of trust in the government was 77.54 per cent, ranking third globally.

Finns who have lived abroad believe that the twentieth-century American dream of stable, prosperous lives is failing. Finnish social scientist Roosa Tikkanen said, "We do not have a culture of brutal competition. In America, it is extreme. People are always worrying, working late, getting sick, insecure, saving money for children's college fees. Finns don't have to worry about all this."

American economist and co-author of the happiness report, Jeffrey D. Sachs observed, "Nordic countries prioritize balance, which is the formula for happiness. They are not societies that are aiming to becoming gazillionaires; they are looking for a good, balanced life and the results are extremely positive." As British politician Ed Miliband famously said, "If you want the American dream, go to Finland."

7

The Role of Public Policy in Generating Happiness

The Indian Experience

"I will give you a talisman. Whenever you are in doubt, or when the self becomes too much with you, apply the following test. Recall the face of the poorest and the weakest man [woman] whom you may have seen, and ask yourself, if the step you contemplate is going to be of any use to him [her]. Will he [she] gain anything by it? Will it restore him [her] to a control over his [her] own life and destiny? In other words, will it lead to swaraj [freedom] for the hungry and spiritually starving millions? Then you will find your doubts and your self melt away."—Mahatma Gandhi

Happiness is the wealth of any nation. Despite its rich cultural heritage, resilience and continuous growth in various domains of development, it is crushing to see that India lies at the 118th position in the World Happiness Index (2025), making it one of the least happy countries in the world out of 147 nations. Happiness is becoming more widely acknowledged as a crucial metric of national well-being that affects both individual lives and the advancement of society at large. In recent years, the value of happiness has grown in popularity, leading several countries to enact policies that put their populations' welfare first. India is no exception.

The *WHR* assesses a number of factors that affect the contentment and well-being of nations. These include:

1. Economic aspects
2. Social support
3. Healthy life expectancy
4. Freedom to choose
5. Generosity
6. Perception of corruption

Importantly, research has shown that while income has a clear effect on happiness, it only accounts for 1 per cent of the population's variance in happiness. Because of this, the US, which has the highest per capita GDP, is ranked 19th in the *WHR 2019*.

Despite China's rapid development since 1990, numerous surveys indicate that the country's citizens are not happier now than they were back then. Apart from these fundamental areas, the Gallup World Poll assesses a number of other topics, such as participation in civic affairs and political processes known as citizen engagement.

Together, these areas offer a thorough awareness of the variables affecting happiness in many countries and enable a nuanced comprehension of the elements that contribute to well-being at the individual and societal levels. Policymakers who want to increase national happiness must have a thorough understanding of these areas. By concentrating on enhancing particular aspects, countries establish settings that promote increased citizen contentment and well-being.

While GDP concentrates on economic activity inside a nation's boundaries, the gross national happiness index (GHI) offers a more comprehensive view of individuals' well-being by considering a number of happiness-related factors. Developing comprehensive policies that promote economic growth and improve general quality of life requires an understanding of both measurements.

How public policy influences happiness in India

The degree to which public policy can affect people's happiness is up for discussion. Without a doubt, the purpose of the state is to enhance the well-being of its citizens. Instead of focusing only on increasing the GDP or any other economic metric, the government's current goal should be to enhance pleasure. However, it is interesting to note that Bruno S. Frey in his book *Economics of Happiness* has made the statement that the government should not be asked to maximize happiness because they can manipulate the calculation of any aggregate happiness index in their favour as they would have control over the collection and analysis of data. For political reasons, governments in power would never like to come out with a finding that people are unhappy.

Additionally, if a happiness survey is conducted, respondents' answers regarding their subjective level of life satisfaction cannot be trusted because they may be aware that their responses will probably be used for political purposes. As a result, they may alter their behaviour to account for the potential political repercussions.

Regarding politicians, I believe that their primary objective is to win elections and stay in power. They use every tactic possible to gain power by making several populist pledges. Their political actions frequently go counter to the population's long-term interests. The government's policies may be heavily influenced by ideology and may not always reflect the preferences of the populace, which is not the best thing to happen.

This is true everywhere in the world, including in India. Political parties offer numerous freebies, including subsidies, to different segments of the populace in the run-up to elections in an attempt to win their support. For example, when it comes to winning votes, the farmer lobby is crucial. Free power, free water, fixed-price procurement, subsidies for fertilizers and other inputs are all promised by successive political parties. Above all, there has been a recent tendency of giving farmers debt waivers. These actions help the political party win votes from the farmer lobby, but when they take office and have to keep their word, it puts a huge financial strain on the state. The situation turns into a larger budgetary imbalance, which is not a wise choice. In order to cover this expense, governments cut back on funding for crucial programs like health and education.

It is true that a welfare state must create programs that aid the underprivileged, and this is frequently the justification for populist policies. Economists contend that these policies lack sound economic principles. In actuality, though, economic decisions are made within a contextual political framework, and they are frequently excellent politics. It can be argued that not all subsidies are harmful, but they must be appropriately targeted and help the intended recipient. Any government must, however, prioritize the happiness of all of its citizens, so it must use public funds in a way that meet the needs of the greatest number of people and foster a sense of well-being in the community.

I feel that governments have an important role to play in the happiness of its citizens through its framing of public policies. Public policy is closely related to the lives of the people and therefore it is responsible to a large degree for their happiness

Good governance and happiness

It is not as if public policy determines all aspects of the happiness of a society because people are not dependent upon the government for everything. Up until the 1991 reforms, India was a highly regulated nation. Since then, the economy has opened up with less regulation and a more open atmosphere for market forces to operate. However, there are instances of market failure where the government must step in to protect the public interest. In particular, the government's primary job is to provide public goods like health and education, which have a direct impact on people's lives and are hence largely responsible for their sense of well-being. A classic example is the rise in air pollution brought on by industry, which the market is unable to control and which requires government intervention through regulatory actions.

In contrast to many Western democracies, the government still plays a significant role in the majority of economic sectors in India, which is why good governance is a key determinant of the level of pleasure of the country's citizens.

Good governance implies a system where there is minimum government but maximum governance. The state's objective is narrowly focused on areas where the markets fall short and the role of the government is crucial rather than being all-encompassing. If the government intrudes on people's basic right to privacy, they will not be pleased. The public desires a helpful but non-intrusive government. The person is aware of his freedom and is most content in a system in which the government offers protection and essential services but does not control every element of his life. This explains why citizens are often happier when its government is more democratic.

Regimes where democracy is merely surface-level and the system is primarily dictatorial do experience economic growth, but as China has shown, the degree of happiness does not increase in direct proportion to the rate of growth. Looking at the list of the happiest nations, we can see that nations with high democracy or freedom scores are ranked higher in the happiness index. Transparency and accountability in government operations are prerequisites for good governance. In such a system, public policies would be developed after thorough consultation with all stakeholders, sensitive to the evolving demands of the populace and focused on enhancing their welfare. The ability of the government to sense public sentiment and be flexible enough to react to it is a sign of good governance. All procedures should be straightforward rather than complicated by a labyrinth of rules and regulations.

Strong and capable leadership and goal-oriented resource management are synonymous with good governance. The vital significance of honesty and integrity is something that has to be acknowledged. The correlation between a nation's ranking on the happiness index and its position on the corruption index, as determined by Transparency International, reflects this.

Corrupt regimes cause a huge deal of discontent among their citizens, which frequently manifests as protests, strikes and even acts of violence. Corrupt governments typically endure for a while before being overthrown by societal unrest or revolution. People are happy when they believe their government is just, fair, impartial and operating in accordance with the law or the Constitution.

Bureaucracy and happiness

The Indian bureaucracy is accused of creating a maze of unnecessary rules, regulations and processes which make it difficult for citizens to even access the most basic of public services. Officers frequently use their authority to deny rather than to promote the provision of services, and they are callous and unsympathetic. As a government worker, I have first-hand experience with how the system operates. In certain situations, but not always, the accusation against the bureaucracy is true. Officers who take the initiative on their own and have a constructive, problem-solving mindset can speed up government operations and cut through red tape.

The Indian government is aware of this, and as a result, it often repeals outdated legislations and substitutes straightforward procedures for complicated regulations. No doubt this would lead to improvement in the happiness quotient of the citizens. People want a simple and transparent system of contacting the government for any need.

The majority of India's administrative reform commissions have emphasized how important it is for the government to be approachable, accommodating, open and constructive; in other words, citizen-friendly. The three essential aspects emphasized in good governance are transparency, accountability and responsiveness of the administration. Innovations like the citizen's charter have been advocated for this purpose.

The basic objective of the citizen's charter is to empower the citizen in relation to public service delivery.

The Department of Administrative Reforms and Public Grievance(DARPG) of the Government of India initiated the task of coordinating, formulating and operationalizing the citizen's charter. The guidelines for formulating the charter as well as a list of do's and don'ts were communicated to various government departments/organizations to enable them to bring out focused and effective charters. For the formulation of the charter, government agencies at the centre and state levels were advised to constitute a task force with representation from users, senior management and cutting-edge staff.

An illustration of this would be a municipal corporation's citizen charter, which provides information on how residents can file complaints on issues like poor sanitation, erratic water supply or a lack of street lighting. It would provide the concerned officer's name, phone number and email address. In a similar vein, it would provide information on how property tax is computed so that the homeowner may determine his tax obligation and make an online tax payment. It has been my experience in public service that people are delighted if they are given a decent hearing. The work will always have to be done as per rules but there should be a positive intent to help the people.

The expectation of the people is that if they want something which is legal, it should be done without the officialdom creating hindrances. For example, if a crime has been committed, the citizen expects that the FIR shall be written without any hassle. Similarly, if government permission is required for something like construction of a house, the citizen feels happy when the system ensures that this is done in a time-bound manner without forcing him to run from one *sarkari* office to another.

In India, a political party that has been in power for five years typically encounters anti-incumbency and loses the next election. It is true that people in India, where poverty rates are still high and income disparities exist, have much too high expectations of the government and are dissatisfied with the current situation. The majority of people seek government contracts or jobs, yet these opportunities never come. They also think that officers and politicians are aloof and conceited. This is one of the prime reasons why India fares so low in the world happiness index. Without a question, people's level of satisfaction would increase if a government reached out to them and they felt that their issues were being addressed. Elections are won by governments that are capable of doing this.

But despite elections, the great majority of people have grown cynical over time and don't think much will change. People losing faith in the integrity of the electoral process is bad for society. Violence and a shift from a democratic to a more authoritarian system of governance could result from this.

Decentralization of governance and happiness

It is necessary to fortify democratic institutions at the local level. In India, local self-governments must have frequent elections and be given the authority to handle the most basic needs of the populace, in addition to the federal and state governments. People's sense of well-being would increase with democratic decentralization and transfer of power and duty. The Constitution's 73rd and 74th amendments specified that over a dozen functions, including health and education, should be transferred to local bodies; however, all states, with the exception of Kerela, have been hesitant to do so.

Technology in governance and happiness

Technology in governance, whether it be mobile or e-government, has greatly aided in providing services and finding quick solutions to issues. In India, a number of state governments have passed public services acts requiring its staff to take prompt action. The primary benefit of technology is that many services are now available online, eliminating the need for citizens to dash from one place to another. There used to be a lot of concerns about government subsidy leaks and corruption in programs designed to eradicate poverty and create jobs.

The direct online cash benefit transfer scheme has considerably reduced corruption levels. The linking of many beneficiaries with Aadhaar card (unique identification number) has greatly improved the targeting of development schemes by eliminating fraud. The Kisan Samman Nidhi Yojana, which transfers Rs 500 per month to the accounts of landholding farmers, is the clearest illustration of this.

Corruption and happiness

Corruption in government schemes has been a major source of unhappiness. Steps have been taken to curb it and technology has really helped. This is clear from the increasingly faceless systems of income tax assessments, passport issuance and railway reservations.

Corruption will reduce if everything is made transparent and available at the push of a button. The perception about corruption in the government is closely related to the satisfaction of the people. We can safely say that in public affairs if the level of honesty and integrity is high, the level of satisfaction of the citizen would be higher.

Unfortunately, there is an increasing trend of acceptance of corruption and its institutionalization. Today corruption is rampant because it has become a low-risk and high-reward activity.

The policymaker

After my first district posting I felt the happiest when a highly respected member of society commented that I have been able to cut the red tape during my tenure. I made it a point to take government to the people by bringing all the departmental officers with me to a subdivisional headquarter and setting up a camp there to resolve problems of the citizens on the spot. He also complimented me on my honesty. Needless to say, when government servants get appreciation from ordinary citizens, they feel the happiest.

This joy is reciprocal. The citizens also feel happy and heap praise on the officers and shower them with their affection and regards. A general feeling of well-being and satisfaction pervades all around. A civil servant, in my opinion, should not be satisfied with maintaining the status-quo.

He should, instead, strive to make a difference to the society. He should work with total commitment and aim to transform the society. A civil servant who works along these lines makes self and others around her happy.

Law and order

A citizen's fundamental expectations of the state are security and law and order. Sensational crimes, particularly those involving women, have caused a great deal of anxiety and uproar in India in recent years. If such crimes are frequently committed, people have a lot of pent-up wrath and fury, and they want the authorities to move quickly to apprehend those who commit such heinous crimes. Police are frequently reluctant to intervene when an important individual is involved, which might result in violent situations.

People are unhappy if the crime rate in their city or district is on the higher side. I recall when I was the district magistrate of a district which was known to be a den of mafias and organized crime, many had shifted their families to some other city out of fear and frustration. The chief minister gave us explicit instructions on how to handle the matter while guaranteeing his full support. My superintendent of police was a superb officer, and we both used every legal authority at our disposal to apprehend these criminals and, where necessary, seize their belongings. After several months of persistent efforts, most of the significant offenders were imprisoned, while many more simply fled the district.

This action of the administration was greatly appreciated by the media, citizens and even politicians. People began to freely move around after sunset and economic activities in the district, which had been curtailed, began to operate in full swing.

The fact that many residents who had fled to nearby places and locked up their homes and businesses returned to the district, as well as the fact that property prices, which had plummeted, stabilized and started to rise, were indicators of this improvement in the situation. All officers of the district were really satisfied with this. I also felt a deep sense of satisfaction.

Similarly, when serious law and order situations erupt in cities, which could be due to communal, caste, student or labour unrest citizens feel insecure and there is a loss of faith in the government. Such situations, if not nipped in the bud, lead to rioting and violence, causing loss of human lives and damage to both public and private property. The tense atmosphere in the district affects the sense of public well-being.

It is for this reason that it is important that the government has a zero tolerance for any disruption of law and order, and concerned officers are held responsible for maintaining peace and harmony in society. If such disruption does occur in spite of all the measures taken, it should be dealt with sternly, impartially and fairly. This is all the more important in communal situations where it is important for the administration to show that they are acting in good faith and not favouring any community.

Compared to serious crimes, minor crimes frequently cause individuals to feel more uneasy. In my experience, instances of chain snatching, eve teasing and *goondaism* (hooliganism) leave an extremely bad impression on people. The moment the police acts in these matters and instils fear in the minds of these petty criminals, citizens feel more secure and are generally satisfied with how the government operates.

The criminal justice system's ability to control crime and maintain peace and order is crucial. This procedure frequently takes an excessively lengthy time in India, which undermines public faith. First of all, filing a first information report (FIR) is difficult for the police. The explanation offered for this is that they want to confirm the facts before filing a formal complaint, but the truth is that there is a natural tendency for police to refrain from filing complaints because they are judged on the quantity of crimes that are committed.

The complainant is naturally upset and unhappy about this. In my experience, when a complainant came to me and I told them to record a formal complaint, they were really satisfied. It is true that crime cannot be completely eradicated, but if it is recognized and swift action is taken, the victim may feel somewhat relieved and satisfied.

A trial in the court of law takes a lot of time in India because of the excessive burden of cases and shortage of judicial officers. Years pass, witnesses become antagonistic, and the entire goal of delivering justice is lost when justice is delayed and eventually denied. Therefore, it is essential that public policy concentrate on improving the criminal justice system's responsiveness, timeliness and impartiality. This will significantly increase the public's trust in the state's judicial and executive branches and provide them a stronger sense of security so they may lead safer, happier lives.

Good law and order attracts investments because no investor would like to put his money where it is not secure. There is, thus, a clear correlation between better law and order and economic growth, and this is why this does become the prime concern of public policy.

Civic sense and happiness

These may appear to be small issues but they have a bearing on citizens' quality of life. Fair and unbiased enforcement of laws with a polite face can certainly lead to law-abiding behaviour. Sometimes, people are not sensitive to the nuisance they might be causing to others because of their behaviour. One instance of this is when music or hymns are blasted through loudspeakers in the middle of the night, creating noise pollution and preventing neighbours from sleeping. This lack of concern for others should be corrected by the education system but this process may take a long time and it is the duty of the law enforcement agencies to take immediate action in these matters.

A society in which citizens are conscious of their accountability towards maintaining the cleanliness of public spaces would certainly be a much happier one than one where there is complete lack of discipline.

SDGs and happiness

We have discussed these goals in some detail in the earlier chapter but there are some goals which stand out as having a direct and forceful relationship with happiness.

Freedom from hunger

At the top of the ladder, I would like to place freedom from hunger. It is just not possible to talk about happiness to hungry people. In my opinion, the first aim of public policy should be to eliminate hunger. As Mahatma Gandhi aptly said, "To a man with an empty stomach, food is god."

The area of focus would have to be generation of employment for all so that they can maintain a minimum standard of living. It is a duty of the government to step in and provide a safety net through either unemployment doles or rural employment guarantee scheme which seeks to provide minimum 100 days of employment to those who desire it at the basic minimum wage rate.

This scheme has been found to be very helpful in India in ensuring that nobody goes to bed hungry. Food production has to be the focus of governments so that enough is produced to meet the food requirements of the people. The government has to support farmers, to incentivize them to use fertilizers, high-yielding variety seeds and other technological inputs to improve productivity. Measures have to be taken to see that farmers get the right price for their produce. The cropping pattern has to be designed scientifically.

Mere food production is not sufficient and it has to ensure that this food is distributed to all sections of the society. In India the public distribution system is used to make this possible by procuring foodgrains from farmers and then distributing them to the poor at subsidized rates. At the time of natural calamities like a drought and floods the government steps in by providing additional quantity of foodgrains to the poor and often this distribution is done free of cost. The Indian government has implemented several initiatives to provide free foodgrains to the poor during the COVID-19 pandemic. One of the most significant measures was the Pradhan Mantri Garib Kalyan Anna Yojana (PMGKAY), which was launched in April 2020. This scheme aimed to distribute 25 kg bowls of cereal per family per month to those affected by the pandemic. The offtake of grains under the National Food Security Act (NFSA) and PMGKAY combined reached 87.5 million metric tonnes in FY21, significantly increasing the availability of foodgrains to the poor.

In India, children coming from poor families have a problem of learning in schools because they do not get proper nutritious meals at home. The Indian government has launched a programme to provide free midday meals to children in schools, which greatly enhanced the attendance, enrolment and learning competencies. To ensure that no one experiences hunger, the government offers a number of pension plans for the elderly and impoverished. However, it is still a matter of concern that in 2025 the rank of India in the global hunger index (GHI) is as low as 102 out of 123 countries. This is a serious matter of concern for public policy in India. If we analyse the global hunger index, we find that it includes weightage for malnutrition and undernutrition which are responsible for bringing down the rank for India. We still have a problem of stunting and wasting, which needs to be addressed by policymakers on an urgent basis. The current GHI projection for the entire world indicates that it would be challenging to achieve the goal of eliminating hunger by 2030, and in 47 countries in particular, the situation is quite serious. The recent COVID outbreak and harsh occurrences linked to global climate change have made food security more difficult. It is surprising that according to GHI the global prevalence of undernourishment after declining for decades has started rising. This indicates a growth in inequalities between regions, countries, district and communities. Africa, South Sahara and South Asia are the world regions where hunger levels are the highest and urgent policy measures are required.

Even though India's rank in the GHI has gone down, the government has been making concerted efforts at improving nutrition to address hunger levels. A national food security act has been formulated which legally entitles 75 per cent of rural population and 50 per cent of urban population to receive subsidized foodgrains under the targeted public distribution system. Food fortification measures have been taken and Poshan Abhiyaan (nutrition mission) was launched in 2018 to tackle the problem of malnutrition.

Integrated child development services are in existence to cater to the needs of children in the age group of 0 to 6 years and pregnant women and lactating mothers. If you want to make people happy, this is a crucial area of public policy that requires constant attention. People who are malnourished or hungry can never have a high happiness quotient.

Freedom from poverty

Poverty also debases human civilization. The eradication of poverty by 2030 is another very important SDG goal. Human society cannot be considered happy if people suffer from poverty, which does not give them basic dignity of living a decent life. There is no doubt that this is a major thrust area of public policy and all governments have been focusing on ways and means of reducing poverty.

Absolute poverty in India, which is defined as earning $1.9 per day in terms of purchasing power parity, has virtually vanished. Even if poverty has decreased over time, various estimations indicate that there is still much work to be done if poverty is to be eradicated. According to a report by Azim Premji University, the COVID-19 epidemic has pushed 230 million (23 crore) individuals below the poverty line.

The stark reality of this situation made the government of India implement special free ration scheme for the poor, which was quite effective in helping them deal with the new circumstances.

Most economists argue that public policy must focus on increasing the rate of growth which by itself will have a trickledown effect on poverty reduction. This is true to a large extent if you look at the data for the Indian economy where there was a high period of growth between 2004–05 and 2012–13, and this corresponded with the maximum reduction in poverty. However, as we have seen in our earlier discussions, growth has also led to increase in inequalities. Other metrics, such as the HDI and GNH, help us enumerate the reality of poverty and provide a better picture of life satisfaction.

Poverty is also a multidimensional concept. It encompasses indicators of health, education and nutrition in addition to income level and food availability. However, our first target is to eliminate absolute poverty so that basic minimum needs of food, shelter and clothing are met. This is a minimum we have to achieve for the entire population by 2030, failing which it would be a mockery to talk about happiness and well-being of the people.

Ensuring proper healthcare

We have seen that poor health is a major cause of unhappiness in an individual and the same applies to the nation where the public health facilities need to be improved in a big way. There is a huge shortage of doctors, nurses and paramedics. More hospitals need to be constructed. Telemedicine must close the gaps and help by providing quality healthcare in remote areas. Every level of the healthcare industry needs to adopt new technology and upgrade ambulance services.

Infant mortality rates and maternal mortality rates are still on the higher side in India and need concerted action. The situation in some states like Uttar Pradesh and Madhya Pradesh is quite alarming. The southern states fare slightly better. If we are to work towards achieving national happiness, India's health policy must address these geographical disparities. The central government should spend at least 2.5 per cent of its GDP on healthcare. Public health must be the top priority when it comes to public policy issues over the next 10 years. In order to have a happy society, we must create a healthy society.

Ensuring equitable and inclusive education

Education is another vital area of public policy. A society which can provide good-quality education to its citizens will definitely be a happier one. Educated citizens develop self-confidence and are able to make choices regarding their well-being. The educated are also aware of their rights and are able to participate effectively in the democratic process of governance. Moreover, education is the gateway to better employment which provides better income and standard of living, both of which are essential for life satisfaction.

India has to go a long distance in making quality education available to its children. Government schools in rural areas suffer from the problems of shortage of teachers, teacher absenteeism, indifference of parents, inadequate infrastructure and lack of hope which are the causes of low enrolment, attendance and learning levels. Additionally, dropout rates are an issue of concern. It is clear that children's median educational attainment and happiness are closely related, and India needs to invest a lot of resources and enhance its governance to achieve this.

The gross enrolment ratio in higher education is barely 26.3 per cent which the new education policy hopes to increase to 50 per cent by 2035. This is essential for the demographic dividend of India to become a reality and provide a better quality of life to the people. This growth might be difficult to achieve since it would necessitate building a lot more colleges, establishing a lot of universities, hiring more professors and improving the infrastructure for education as a whole. It becomes imperative for the government to spend up to 6 per cent of its GDP on education. It is through education that citizens will be able to grow, develop their personality, bring out their latent talents and make a positive impact on society. It is tool for empowerment.

Many young boys and girls in rural India today have dropped out of school or college for a variety of reasons and have very few aspirations for the future. All Indians should have access to high-quality education so they may make informed decisions about their life. As public goods, health and education ought to be India's top objectives.

Ensuring productive unemployment and decent work

One of the major causes of unhappiness is the level of unemployment in the country. Nothing is more detrimental to a person's physical and mental health than being unable to find employment to support oneself or one's family, or having a job that underemploys them and does not allow them to develop their inner talents. Surprisingly, the experience of India has demonstrated that although the economy's growth rate increased continuously following the 1991 economic reforms, the rate of employment growth did not match this.

One of the reasons has been that there has been a slow movement of people from farm to non-farm occupations because the pace of growth of the manufacturing sector has been less than desired. Even the growth that has taken place has been more capital than labour intensive because of the existence of archaic labour laws which make it almost impossible to do away with labour whose performance is poor and leads to low productivity. Generally speaking, governments have shown support for labour unions, which have been unable to align their future with the industry's.

I remember working in a public sector business where it was impossible to fire offending employees even after acts of aggression against management were discovered. After conducting an investigation, dismissal orders were issued; however, the labour court intervened to overturn these orders and put the management in a humiliating position.

This is one of the primary causes of the poor performance of public sector manufacturing firms.

Implementing labour reforms

However, even the private sector has to face similar situations though they are in a better position to act than the public sector. I personally experienced a labour unrest situation in a famous automotive company in Lucknow in the late 1990s when I was serving as the secretary to the chief minister. Some bad elements had manhandled a few engineers in the factory and when the management terminated their services, they took the help of the unions to go on a strike.

It so happened that one of the unions was affiliated to the labour wing of the ruling party and they put pressure on the chief minister to reinstate the errant employees. This was unacceptable to TATA Motors' management, who stated that they would prefer to cease operations in Uttar Pradesh than put up with such hooliganism.

I had to make every effort to persuade the chief minister that the government's response to the crisis would determine the state's interests and economic future. As a result, the government adopted a firm stance and backed the management. Law and order was upheld, and the factory restarted after the unions realized how powerful the state was. This delivered a strong message to the whole industrial sector, encouraging them to continue operating and making investments in Uttar Pradesh.

However, it is not that the safety and security concerns of the labour should be overlooked. There are several instances where capitalists exploit workers, and there are even instances where fundamental safety regulations are neglected and minimum wages are not provided. It is thus advisable to strike a balance between the interest of labour and management and this could be done by developing institutional mechanisms. Additionally, workers must be persuaded that the expansion of the manufacturing sector is directly related to their future, as this is likely to result in high employment and, thus, happiness.

The Indian government has recently worked on labour reforms by eliminating out-of-date legislations and consolidating all labour-related laws that were scattered throughout numerous acts and regulations into four labour codes. This is a welcome move but much more is required to be done to ensure that employment levels rise and there is no exploitation of labour. If such an ecosystem is developed, labour-intensive manufacturing will expand and reverse the trend of growth without employment.

Employment policy

The pandemic was a great shock and because of recurring lockdowns, industries decided to lay off workers, leaving them to fend for themselves. As a result, large groups of migrant workers and their families were observed returning thousands of miles to their villages. One of the main causes of discontent in society was the unemployment that the epidemic brought about, which resulted in widespread suffering.

Although this was a global occurrence, India suffered the most due to its sizable labour force. It will take some time for the effects to fade. Employment programs that specifically target the most vulnerable groups will undoubtedly aid in easing the suffering and eliminating the source of discontent.

Demographic dividend

With over 60 per cent of its people in the working age group, India is currently experiencing a demographic dividend. If appropriate employment is not available, this might become a curse and hinder the country's progress. The country's economy would grow more quickly and there would be peace and stability if these young people's energies are directed in a constructive way through employment.

I would like to mention that the level of unemployment in the educated youth has been on the higher side leading to voices of protests at the street level with young boys and girls turning towards crime due to frustration. The educated youth are much more outspoken, and if they are unemployed, it will have a cascading effect on society as a whole, leading to conflict and social unrest. It is, thus, imperative for policymakers take steps to mitigate unemployment.

The Mahatma Gandhi National Rural Guarantee Act (MGNREGA) has greatly aided job seekers in rural India who would not otherwise be able to find productive employment. This act stipulates that a job card holder will have access to up to 100 days of work every calendar year. It is also a key tool for aid during extreme droughts and other natural disasters. Strangely, the threat of widespread unemployment is still very much present. This scheme has now been replaced by a new employment scheme called VB-G-RAMG. Different viewpoints are there on whether it will be an improvement on MGNREGA.

India has not taken into account the necessity of creating an employment policy that would have allowed for thorough monitoring of the country's unemployment rate and kind. I am convinced that the level of unemployment and the level of unhappiness are directly linked to one another. It is, thus, the primary duty of the state to have an employment policy and to see that the youth get the employment which it is looking for.

Achieving gender equality

The degree of happiness in society is greatly impacted by gender issues in public policy. Women's labour force participation rates in India are extremely low, which has been a significant barrier to both the rate of economic progress and the degree of subjective well-being. Indian policymakers need to take this issue seriously. If they can provide a framework that allows women to reach their full potential and find lucrative employment, the country's citizens will undoubtedly have higher levels of life satisfaction.

Gender awareness must be implanted in young people's minds from an early age, and gender budgeting is another notion that can be used when choosing how to use public resources. An increasing number of girls will benefit from education, which will provide them the tools to lead meaningful lives. There is a direct correlation between the education of girls and various health indicators like infant mortality rate, maternal mortality rate and total fertility rate.

Many Indian children are experiencing the negative consequences of malnutrition, such as stunting and wasting, as a result of women's lack of awareness, low levels of education and poor health. If the objective of public policy is to create happiness, the focus on the well-being of women is perhaps one of the most vital aspects that should concern the policymaker.

Ensuring responsible production

Although 15 per cent of India's GDP comes from agriculture, the sector employees 45 per cent of the workforce and is the primary cause of rural poverty. These figures are even starker if you consider the populous yet backward regions of Uttar Pradesh and Bihar. I have served in the government in Uttar Pradesh for almost 40 years and even now this sector contributes to 25 per cent of the state domestic products and 65 per cent of the people still subsist on agriculture. As a result, the land holdings have become so dispersed that 86 per cent of farmers are small and marginal, making farming unfeasible for them.

To guarantee that farmers receive a fair return on their investments, the government must intervene to offer subsidies for fertilizers, seeds and technology as well as assistance through minimum support price operations. The main structural changes that public policy must address in order to lessen farmer suffering are agricultural marketing reforms. Mechanisms have to evolve to ensure that farmers get a remunerative price for their produce. Cooperatives and farmer-producer businesses are examples of aggregation models that would greatly strengthen farmers and improve their ability to adapt to market fluctuations.

There is no doubt the policies related to the farmers influence results of the elections in the country and it is because of this that this sector has attracted the focus of the politicians and the public policymakers. If public policy is able to wean away the excess labour from farm occupations to non-farm jobs, the nation would develop much more quickly and provide more welfare for everyone, which will increase life happiness.

Sustainable development and happiness

Public policy today is indeed focused on sustainable development, which encompasses the integration of economic, social and environmental considerations. Large-scale road construction often leads to widespread cutting of trees or displacement of people and the acquisition of agricultural land. It is for this reason that the social and environmental cost of any project has to be taken into account while deciding the feasibility or viability of the project. Public policy must ensure that resources are preserved for future generations. Clean water and air need to be conserved.

Furthermore, climate change has become a major factor in policymaking. Countries were asked to indicate when they will achieve net zero emissions during the international climate change summit COP 26 in 2022. Fossil fuels have to be phased out and the share of renewable resource of energy has to increase substantially. At the international level, this has become a bone of contention between developed and developing countries. India, which belongs to the latter category, has boldly stated that while it is dedicated to reaching the decarbonization goals, it is unable to comply with a hard deadline.

India has pledged to significantly increase its proportion of renewable energy, but it has set a deadline for reaching net zero only after 2060. Industrialized nations should take the lead in achieving net zero since they have the biggest per capita emissions of greenhouse gases. Developing nations like India must strike a compromise between the need to reduce greenhouse gas emissions and the urgency of achieving greater economic growth. Each nation must determine how to strike a balance between the two goals, each of which is crucial.

They have to weigh short-term happiness of their people with achieving long-term life satisfaction and eventually a better quality of growth. The needs of the present and future generations have both to be taken into account. In order to attain this balance, the UN developed the SDGs, which are covered in more detail in another chapter.

The COVID-19 pandemic and happiness

The pandemic caused a lot of unhappiness all over the world. There was a sense of fear and dread in society as cases and mortalities multiplied on a daily basis. Developed countries suffered as much less developed one. People were forced into lockdowns in their houses with little social contact with the outside world, leading to domestic tension and depression.

The work culture underwent a big change with people working from home instead of going to offices leading to a negative impact on team building and group working which are essential to enhance the productivity of an organization. The worst affected were children as schools were shut down and online classes started which were not a good substitute for the school environment. This not only reduced the learning levels but also caused mental health issues for many children. Due to a lack of internet connectivity, impoverished children in rural India were unable to attend online lessons, which caused them to lag behind in their learning competencies. A lot of effort is now being made to remedy the situation but many children who left school during the pandemic are yet to come back, causing a negative impact on their future well-being.

In India, the second wave of the COVID-19 epidemic was particularly devastating since there was a shortage of oxygen cylinders, ICU beds, ventilators and medications, with death being a constant threat in practically every home. This period exposed the limitations of our public health infrastructure. Although the crisis has subsided, it has brought attention to public health and the need for public policy to develop plans of action and strategies to significantly increase the number and quality of health services in order to prevent future occurrences of this kind of issue. In response, the federal and state governments of India have increased the budgetary allotment for the health care sector.

Facilitating role of public policy

Another crucial issue pertaining to public policy is whether the state should directly handle the issues of the less fortunate segments of society or concentrate on fostering an atmosphere that allows economic activity to occur without entering the market. Since growth and equity have long been at odds, public policy has started emphasizing on metrics like GNH and HDI.

With the exception of certain instances of market failure where government intervention is necessary, markets can be trusted to produce the best distribution of resources. Some of the major causes of market failure are externalities, asymmetry of information, monopolies and the case of public goods.

For instance, we would prefer that supply and demand in the market determine the production of goods and services. While this may seem ideal, there may be a negative externality to manufacturing growth, such as air pollution, which the market is unable to address and would necessitate state policy intervention.

Similarly, if there is no perfect competition and monopolies or oligopolies exist, the market fails and the state must step in by creating public policies that encourage competition for the benefit of the populace. Finally, for public goods like law and order, security, and health and education the state has to provide these as the private sector is not in a position to do the same optimally.

Citizen-centric policy and effective execution

The ultimate goal of public policy is the well-being of the people and thus it has to be citizen-centric and outcome-oriented. To make this happen not only have proper policies to be designed in consultation with all the stakeholders but the policy has to be implemented in a proper manner and has to be regularly evaluated. If the evaluation shows that the goals of the policy are not being met, feedback should be shared with policymakers who should accordingly reframe policies.

Implementation of public policy has to be kept in mind at the time of policy formulation so that the policy does not remain a mere utopian statement of intent. In fact, each policy should have a detailed action plan for implementation and it is the duty of civil servants and other government officials to efficiently and effectively implement it so that the goals are met in the required timeframe. This requires quality leadership.

Aligning everyone with the objective, fostering teamwork and team spirit, making decisions quickly, inspiring and motivating others, communicating effectively and keeping an eye on things are all components of leadership. Leadership would have to get the best out of people which is an art by itself.

If the people involved in implementation in public policy are motivated properly, they will go about their task in a happy frame of mind. Additionally, citizens who receive the benefits of a well-executed program are extremely happy since they don't have to run from pillar to post for them.

System of grievance redressal and happiness

The ability to voice their concerns to government officials and political leaders and the existence of a grievance redressal system that satisfactorily addresses their concerns, enhances the happiness of citizens. I would emphasize that effective grievance redressal is the cornerstone of a public policy ecosystem which leads to overall life satisfaction in the people.

People want to get a fair hearing and that is why it is important for government officials to listen to them. The ability to listen is uncommon and goes much beyond just hearing. Empathy, compassion and understanding are all components of listening.

Corruption and public policy

Nothing causes more unhappiness than corruption in the delivery of public services. This problem is endemic to the Indian scenario also. In order to provide services to the public in a fair and unbiased manner and to ensure that public funds are used for the purpose for which they are intended, public policy should strive to eradicate corruption. Political corruption is the fountainhead of all corruption in India with government officials illegally amassing wealth at the expense of ordinary citizens. Strangely, corruption is on the rise despite an increase in the agencies investigating it.

The reason behind this is growing materialism in society which has led to a degradation of values in society in general especially among government servants. Societies where there is low level of corruption are happier than those where corruption is rampant, institutionalized and accepted. Technology can be a game changer and corruption can be reduced significantly through e-governance and m-governance.

Taxation and happiness

Increasing resources is a crucial component of public policy, and tax increases typically elicit the strongest response from the populace. A higher income tax means a lower disposable income which also means a lesser capacity to buy desired goods and services. However, the state cannot possibly provide services to people unless they have the mandate to collect taxes and utilize the same for the benefit of the people. High and direct taxes like import duties raise the price level of imported goods in the market causing uneasiness among citizens.

More than these taxes, it is the municipal taxes, for example property tax, local sales tax, that cause a lot of resentment in society because the citizen feels their immediate and direct impact. However, one of the most important tasks of public policy is to raise resources. The state may appear coercive in doing so but there can be no provision of merit goods like education, healthcare, without the required quantity of resources being made available.

Citizens pay close attention to the Government of India's annual budget each year, particularly to see if the tax rates or slabs have changed. There will be a general sense of contentment and well-being in the nation if there is no tax rise.

Somehow, people want lower taxes but also want the government to provide security, health and education. This is true not only for India but in most countries where politicians win elections by proposing tax cuts if they come to power. Happiness is linked to taxation in a country with a high tax rate leading to misery.

India had a highly harsh tax system back in the 1970s, with about 97.5 per cent of income taxed at the highest income level. This caused a lot of dissatisfaction and also acted as a disincentive for the private sector to invest, having a negative impact on the level of economic growth. It also fostered the growth of black money, with rampant tax evasion.

The making of public policy

It is incumbent for the public servant to do proper planning and develop systems to implement public policy better. A well-administered public policy ecosystem is an essential requirement to create happiness in society. Public policy is a complex issue and should not be done in a hurry. The more the deliberation at the policy formulation stages the higher the chances of the policy to be successful. In their insightful book, *In the Service of the Republic*, Vijay Kelkar and Ajay Saha offer an intriguing perspective on policymaking by comparing it to a five-day Test match rather than a T20.

They also say that it is important to feel the stones underneath while crossing the river. I must also point out that public policy is a dynamic concept and the policy paper on any issue has to provide answers to real-life issues. It should, thus, be open to feedback of any kind and there should be no rigidity in accepting that something is not working and needs to be changed. By creating a system for regularly tracking happiness indicators, policymakers can gain a better understanding of the effectiveness of programs that have been put into place. Priority should be given to feedback mechanisms that enable citizens to express concerns about policies that impact their well-being.

Public policies are formulated by the political executive on the basis of the advice rendered to them by the civil servant. The job of the civil servant is to give fair and frank advice so that the policy formulated is in accordance with the law of the land and also beneficial to the people. The political executive is in a better position to feel the pulse of the people and it is their job to give a vision to policymaking. For effective policymaking, the civil servant is well within his rights to disagree with the directions of the political dispensation.

However, once a policy is finalized it is the job of the civil servant to implement it faithfully and effectively. If the civil servant is able to implement the policy efficiently, it leads to development of the society and redressal of grievances of the people. The relationship between the civil servant and the political is complementary, like wheels of a vehicle, and they must move in tandem to give the best results.

The civil servants must be chosen on the basis of merit and trained to be open, accessible, transparent, fair, accountable, result-oriented and responsive to the public in order to achieve optimal implementation and results. In order to guarantee that only officers with competence and integrity advance to the higher levels of the service, the performance evaluation system for civil workers should be impartial and focused on merit. Above all, the civil servant must be sensitive to the needs and the aspirations of the weaker and underprivileged sections of society.

The next step after implementing a public policy is to evaluate it to see if its objectives have been achieved. Instead of relying solely on the data supplied by the implementing agency, this might be accomplished by engaging a third party. Independent assessments of the policy can be carried out by NGOs, non-profits, academic institutions and civil society. The idea is to get a proper feedback and amend the policy document so that public policy genuinely addresses the problems. Only then will it be able to give people a satisfactory quality of life.

The happiness research in which economists have recently become engaged constitutes an important advance over previous economics. This research is only in its initial stages, and much still awaits analysis. For instance, most happiness studies consider developed economies. Additional empirical studies devoted to developing economies could broaden the picture and qualify previous findings. It has sometimes been claimed that comparisons of happiness between countries make little sense because of cultural differences. While differences between cultures are important, they are often exaggerated. Culture may, to some extent, affect what factors influence happiness but, as shown in various studies, there are universal factors determining subjective well-being, and it may also be argued that happiness as an ultimate goal in life is independent of culture.

We can conclude by reiterating that the pursuit of public policy should be to make its citizens happy. Sometimes bold decisions have to be taken which may cause immediate discomfort but but in hindsight they might turn out for the better of the people. Optimizing public welfare is perhaps the most important goal of public policy. Happiness of the people has to be the cherished goal of public policy. In the end, happiness should be seen as a shared objective that represents the well-being of society as a whole, rather than only as an individual endeavour. It was none other than the great J.R.D. Tata who famously said, "I do not want India to be an economic super power. I want it to be happy".

Bibliography

Ayyar, R.V.V. (2009). *Public Policymaking in India*. India: Pearson.

Brooks, Arthur C. (2008). *Gross National Happiness*. United States: Basic Books.

Brinkerhoff, M. B., K. Fredell and J.S. Friders (1997). "Basic minimum needs, quality of life and selected correlates: Explorations in villages in Northern India." *Social Indicators Research*, 42, 245–281. https://doi.org/10.1023/A:1006834830518

Dalai Lama (1999). *The Art of Happiness: A Handbook for Living*. UK: Hodder Paperbacks.

Diener, E. (1984). "Subjective Wellbeing." *Psychological Bulletin*, 95, pp. 542–575.

Diener, E. and M.E.P. Seligman (2004). "Beyond Money: Toward an Economy of Well-being." *Psychological Science in the Public Interest*, 5, 1–31.

Diener, E. and R. Biswas-Diener (2008). *Unlocking the Mysteries of Psychological Wealth*. Malden, MA: Wiley/ Blackwell.

Frey, Bruno S. and Alois Stutzer (2001). *Happiness and Economics: How the Economy and Institutions Affect Human Well-Being*. United Sates: Princeton University Press.

Kelkar, Vijay and Ajay Shah (2019). *In Service of the Republic: The Art and Science of Economic Policy*. India: Penguin.

Lyubomirsky, S. (2013). *The Myths of Happiness: What Should Make You Happy, but Doesn't, What Shouldn't Make You Happy, But Does*. New York, NY: Penguin.

Maddison, Angus (2007). *Contours of the World Economy 1-2030 Ad: Essays in Macro-economic History*. UK: Oxford University Press.

Pilling, David (2019). *The Growth Delusion*. United Kingdom: Bloomsbury

Ricard, Matthieu (2015). *Happiness: A Guide to Developing Life's Most Important Skill*. United Kingdom: Atlantic Books.

Rojas, Mariano (2019). *The Economics of Happiness: How the Easterlin Paradox Transformed Our Understanding of Well-Being and Progress* (Kindle edition). Springer.

Sachs, Jeffrey D. (2015). *The Age of Sustainable Development*. United States: Columbia University Press.

Seligman, Martin (2004). *Authentic Happiness: Using the New Positive Psychology to Realize Your Potential for Lasting Fulfillment*. United Kingdom: Nicholas Brealey Publishing.

Shahar-Tal Ben (2007). *Happier: Learn the Secrets to Daily Joy and Lasting Fulfillment*. India: McGraw-Hill Education.

——. (2010). *Being Happy: You Don't Have to Be Perfect to Lead a Richer, Happier Life*. India: McGraw-Hill Education.

Stigtliz, Joseph, Jean-Paul Fitoussi and Martine Durand (2019). *Beyond GDP: Measuring What Counts for Economic and Social Performance.* Organisation for Economic Cooperation and Development (OECD).

Human Development Reports from 1990 to 2025.

World Happiness Reports from 2012 to 2025.

Acknowledgements

I want to start by expressing my gratitude to my parents for providing me with an environment that taught me that happiness in life is contingent upon making others happy. I believe that policymakers and anyone interested in public policy, including students, would find this book to be quite relevant. Those who believe that happiness is the ultimate objective in life should also find it appealing. The science and art of happiness are becoming more and more popular because everyone wants to be happy.

I cannot express enough thanks to my students of Jaipuria Institute of Management, Lucknow, whose overwhelming response to my happiness course motivated me to write this book. I was pleasantly surprised to learn that MBA students could value a non-materialistic outlook on life so highly and so early on in life. I hope that students from different fields will show a similar desire to discover a greater meaning in life.

I have learnt a lot about public policy from political leaders, my senior colleagues in the Indian Administrative Service and the citizens of our great country. I am indebted to them for this.

I am grateful to my dynamic publisher Ajay Mago for having faith in me and my writing and publishing this book. I am overwhelmed by the diligence and involvement of my editor Jyotsna Mehta who gave this book a meaning and a structure. I am immensely thankful to her for the same.

My wife Surabhi, who patiently gave me the time, space and happiness to create this book, has my deepest gratitude.

I thank my readers who have taken an interest in my work. Your encouragement and feedback motivate me to keep exploring and writing.

Thanks are due to my PA, Chandramohan, for diligently typing out the manuscript.

Lastly, I would like to thank all of them whose names are not mentioned here but have helped me in some way to accomplish my work.